Richard Baxter

Naked Popery

Richard Baxter

Naked Popery

ISBN/EAN: 9783337254803

Printed in Europe, USA, Canada, Australia, Japan

Cover: Foto ©Lupo / pixelio.de

More available books at **www.hansebooks.com**

Naked Popery;

OR, THE

NAKED FALSHOOD

Of a Book called the

CATHOLICK NAKED TRUTH,

OR THE

Puritan Convert to Apoſtolical Chriſtianity; Written by *W. H.*

Opening their Fundamental Errour of Unwritten Tradition, and their unjuſt Deſcription of the *Puritan*, the *Prelatical Proteſtant*, and the *Papiſt*, and their differences; and better acquainting the ignorant of the true difference, eſpecially what a *Puritan* and what a *Papiſt* is.

By *RICHARD BAXTER*, a Profeſſor of meer Apoſtolical Chriſtianity.

Trita frequenſq; via eſt per Amici fallere nomen;
Trita frequenſq; licet ſit via, crimen habet.

The common beaten way of mens deceit
Is as a *Loving Friend* to work the Cheat:
But though this be the common beaten way,
It will prove criminal——another day.

W. H. this Author, pag. 25. faith [*If you do not find that——they (your Catholick Neighbours) hold nothing, nor Practiſe nothing, but what they are able to give a very ſatisfactory account of to any impartial Enquirer, then ſay, I am a Knave, a Lyar, and a Cheat, one that deſerveth no mercy from God or Man, in this World or the next.*]

LONDON,
Printed for *N. Simmons* at the Princes Arms in S. *Paul's* Church-Yard. MDCLXXVII.

TO THE
AUTHOR
AND HIS
RELATIONS.

CHAP. I.

WHEN the Confutation of the Treatise of Transubstantiation was in the Press, this Book came to my notice, written, if the Stile may go for Proof, by the *same Author*: It is conjectured that your Name is Mr. *W. Hutchinson* of *Lincolnshire*, sometime of *Queens Colledge* in *Cambridge*; and that it is indeed your nearest Relations whom you so earnestly labour to pervert: Your *Stile* perswadeth me that you are *serious*, and verily think that your way is right: And I suppose you see that we also are as confident of the truth of our Profession, as you are of yours: The Question is, whether it be *your* Zeal, or *ours*, that is according to Knowledge?

The Title of your Religion greatly pleaseth me, and is the same that I assume: For we are, I perceive, agreed in this, that it is [*the Apostolical Christianity*] that is the true and safe Religion: And hath God left the matter so obscure as that we cannot come to an agreement in so weighty a matter of Fact, as to know what [*the Apostolical Christianity*] was; when even Common History giveth us notice what the *Athenian* Philosophers held, and what the ancient *Romans* held, and so of almost every literate Nation? *You* study, and *we* study; *You* pray, and *we* pray: You would know the truth, whatever it cost you, and so would We. As a Man that looketh daily when I am called away to God, I solemnly protest, that if I could find that Popery were the true Apostolick Christianity, I would joyfully quit all the Friends, Hope, and Interests of this World, to embrace it. What is it that is your advantage, and what is our disadvantage? Are you more impartial in your search? I am so Conscious of my Impartiality, that I cannot believe that this maketh the difference. Is it that we have not read the Papists writings? I have reason to believe that I have read as many of them, at least, as you have done, if you are not much above sixty years of age (as I hear you are not near it). But you have Conversed with more of them than I have done? It's like you have: But is that the reason of my mistake? You earnestly invite your Relations to Converse with the Papists, because mens *writings* may be mistaken: And on this ground I perceive you build all the certainty of your Faith, That *our Fathers* and *our Grand-Fathers* have told us Infallibly, what they received from their Fathers and Grand-Fathers, and so on. This is your certainty.

I will tell you briefly what I take for the *Apostolical Christi-*

Christianity, and by what Notices I receive it ; and then I will again consider yours.

I take not *Christianity* to be a thing so hardly to be known, as you would make it; either as to *the Being* of it, or the *Publication*. I take it to have its *Essentials, Integrals*, and *Accidentals* ; and that these are not to be confounded: If it cannot be readily known what Christianity is, how shall we preach it to Heathens ? or how shall Christians be known to others, or themselves? and who can have the comfort of an unknown Religion ?

You tell us that nothing of it is *written* in the New Testament, but the Life of Christ by four Men, and a few occasional Epistles, *&c.* But do you think that Christ himself did not institute Christianity, and tell Men plainly what it was ? Did not those four Men write *Christ's Doctrine* as well as his *Life* ? And is he not the *Author of our Faith* ? Did he not preach the Gospel ? And do you not call these four Books the four Evangelists ? And doth not the Gospel contain and describe Christianity? Did not Christ oft tell us what it is to be his Disciples? And were not the Disciples called Christians shortly after, as words of the same signification ? But what place is there for any doubt, when Christ himself did institute Baptism, and describe it ? and command that all Nations being Discipled should be Baptized into the Name of the Father, the Son, and the Holy Ghost ; as being the Faith which Disciples must profess ? And do not you to this day profess, that Baptizing is Christening, and that Baptism washeth away all sin, (supposing the Baptized to receive it as Baptism, by true Covenant-consent at least ?) And doth not Baptism enter us into the true Church of Christ ? Sure all this is past dispute ; where then is the difficulty ? Is not a truly baptized

zed Person a Christian? And was it then as hard a matter as you make it, to know *what Faith was necessary to Baptism,* (in the Person at age, or the Parent of Infants?) Surely then the Scripture, that mentioneth the History of so many thousands baptized, would have told us of that grand Controversie, and how it was decided. But no such Controversie was then debated, for ought we there find. If Baptismal Covenanting with God the Father, Son, and Holy Ghost, as our God and Father reconciled in Christ, our Saviour, and our Sanctifier, be not the *Symbol* or *Badge* of *Christians*, and that which visibly maketh them such; your own Church, and all the Christian World is deceived. And we know that it was not the Custom of the Apostles and Pastors of the ancient Churches, to make a meer Ceremony and dead Formality of Baptism, by baptizing those that would but say the words [*I believe in God the Father, Son, and Holy Ghost,*] without understanding what they said: And therefore their ordinary Preaching was the Exposition of these three Articles: And the Creed called The Apostles, is the Exposition of these three Articles; which though some Clauses were since added, and though the Churches tyed not themselves just to the very same words, (as we find by the various forms of this Creed in *Irenæus, Tertullian, Marcellus's* in *Epiphanius, Ruffinus, &c.*) yet for the substance and sense, and most of the very words, all Churches used the same. And when the Council of *Nice* taught them the way of making new Creeds, (which *Hilary Pict.* so sadly complaineth of,) yet still the matter of the old Creed was the substance of them all. And the Eastern Creed, which was used before the *Nicene* Council, (for that such a one there was, the most Learned Antiquaries give us sufficient proof,) was but the same in

sense

sense as the Western, even the Exposition of the Baptismal Faith; and this the Baptized did profess before Baptism: And the work of Catechists was to teach this and the sense of it to the Catechumens. And that [*He that believeth and is baptized* (that is, truly devoted to God the Father, Son, and Holy Ghost, by the Baptismal Covenant) *shall be saved, and he that believeth not shall be damned,*] is by Christ himself made the sum of his Gospel, or Law of Grace.

As the Image of the blessed Trinity on mans Soul is *Life, Light,* and *Love*; so the summaries of that sacred Doctrine which must imprint it on us, is the *Symbolum Fidei,* the *Creed,* the summary of things to be *believed*; and the *Lords Prayer,* the *Symbolum* and summary of things to be *willed, desired,* and *sought*; and the *Decalogue,* the summary of *things to be practised*; being the Directory of Mans three Faculties, the *Intellect,* the *will,* and the *Executive Power.* And all this we believe was delivered to the Churches by the Apostles, and received by all Christians, many years (eight at least) before any Book of the New Testament was written: And for the fuller understanding and improvement of it, and for all the integral parts of Religion that were to be added, the Apostles and Evangelists more enlargedly preached them to the People in their Sermons, as Christ himself had done much of them. We receive all that, as Gods Word, which by these Apostles was delivered as such to the Churches; because they had the promise of the Holy Ghost to lead them into all truth, and to bring all things that Christ taught and commanded to their remembrance. We are assured that all that is contained in the *New Testament* was written by such *inspired Persons*; and that the Spirit of God well knew, that when they
were

were to dye, without written Records, the memory of Mankind would not faithfully retain, and deliver to Posterity, such copious matter as the *Integrals* and useful *Accidentals* of Religion, and therefore caused them to write it and leave it to Posterity.

So that our Christian Religion is contained and delivered to us in *three Formulas* or *Prescripts*: The *first* containeth the *whole Essence of Christianity*, and is the *Sacramental Covenant*, in which we are believingly given up to God the *Father, Son, and Holy Ghost*, and God to us, in the Relation of a God and Father, a Saviour and a Sanctifier. This is done initially, *ad esse*, in Baptism, and after *ad robur* in the *Lords Supper*. This is delivered to us by *Tradition Naturally Infallible, de facto*: For *all Christians, as such*, have received and entred this *Sacramental Covenant*; and full History assureth us, that the very same Form of it is come down in all the Churches to this day.

The second *Formula*, is the *Exposition* of the three Articles of this Sacramental Covenant, in the *Creed, Lords Prayer*, and *Decalogue*; which hath been delivered by memory also, and kept unchanged (save the foresaid additions of some explicatory words in the *Creed*,) to all the Churches to this day.

The third *Form*, is *all the holy Canonical Scriptures*, (the Old Testament being as preparatory to the New,) which contain all the *Essentials, Integrals, and needful Accidentals*.

Our Religion then is all from Christ and his Spirit, in inspired men, commissioned to deliver it, and is well called as you do, the *Apostolical Christianity*: We own no other. It is all brought down to us by Tradition from the Apostles. The *Essentials* in the Covenant, and the explicatory

explicatory Symbols or Summaries, are delivered to us two ways: First by *Memory and Practice* most currant and certain from Generation to Generation, being no more than what Memory might well retain, whereto yet the helps of the *Ancients writings* reciting the Forms were used for the fuller certainty of Posterity. Secondly in the *holy Scriptures*, where they are contained (as the *Brain, Heart,* and *Stomach,* in the Body) among all the rest as the *Principal* Parts. The third form is so large that Memory could not preserve it, and therefore God would have it delivered us in that Writing which we all call the Sacred Bible, or Canonical Scripture. This containeth thousands of words more than are of absolute necessity to Salvation; but no more than is useful or helpful to Salvation.

In all this I have shewed you what our Religion is, (*Objectively* taken) and which way we receive it. Where you are therefore to note, 1. That all our Sermons, Writings, Church-Articles, *&c.* are but the Expressions of our *Subjective Religion,* telling other Men how particular Men, and particular Churches, understand those *Divine Forms* which are our *Objective* Religion: These are various as Churches and Persons are, every one having his own Faith and Religion in different measures, and such expressions being but our *fides mensurata* may be altered and amended, and we pretend not to perfection in them: But the former being our *fides vel Religio mensurans,* our *Divine Objective* Faith or Religion, is inculpable and unalterable.

2. Note that *you Papists* do grant all *our Objective Faith and Religion,* even every word of it, to be *true, infallible, and of God*: You own, I say, every word of *our Religion:* That is, all the *Sacramental Covenant,* all the

B   Creed,

Creed, Lords Prayer, and Decalogue, and all that which we call the holy *Canonical Scriptures.* But we own not all yours: So that you do not, you cannot find fault with the least Particle of our Religion as to the truth of it; but, 1. You think that it is not *enough*: And 2. That we come not to it the right way, that is, we take not our Faith upon the word of Papists, as Papists. Is not this the difference? And is not this all that you cry out against us for?

And now let us see whether your way be better and surer than this of ours is?

I. Your Religion is much Bigger than ours.

II. You hold it on other Reasons, and plead another way of receiving it.

I. Your Religion (Objective) containeth, besides all our Bible, all the *Apocryphal Books,* and all the *Decrees of General Councils,* and all the other *un-written Traditions* (if there be any more, who knows what?) you name your self here, *fasting on Frydays, and on the vigils of Saints, Ember-days, Lent, and Images,* and such like.

Here now we humbly propose to your consideration; 1. Whether you will take all these into the *Essentials of Christianity,* or not? If not, a Man may be *a Christian*; and consequently of the Church, or Body of Christ, and in a state of Salvation without them. Why then do you deny them this, and make them to be as out of the true Church and state of Life? If yea,

Q. 2. Did all that the Apostles Baptized, believe all the *Apocrypha* and all the *Decrees of your Councils,* and your Oral Traditions?

Q. 3. Did the ancient Fathers and Catechists teach all those to the Catechumens before they Baptized them?

Q. 4. And were not those all Christians, and in the

true

true Church, and in a state of Life, whom the Apostles Baptized, without the profession of any such Belief?

Q. 5. What was the *Creed*, the *Symbolum fidei* used for, if not to distinguish the Faith of the Christian Church from Infidelity, Heresie, and all without? And if all the Decrees of Councils be as necessary to be the *Symbol of Faith*, why were they not all made up into a Creed? and why is the Creed differenced from them all to this day? And why do you not cause the Baptized to recite and profess all these Councils Decrees, but only the old Christian Creed?

Q. 6. Doth not Christ at the Institution of his Sacrament, *Mat.* 28. expresly promise that *he that believeth* (according to Baptism, in the *Father, Son, and Holy Ghost*) *shall be saved*?

Q. 7. Is it not a reproach to God and the Christian Religion, to tell the World that God hath written us by his Spirit so great a Book as the Bible is, and yet there is not in it enough to Salvation, but that abundance *unnecessary* to Salvation is in it, and some necessary things left out?

Q. 8. Have your Oral superadded Traditions more *Evidence of Truth than the Bible*, or more *Evidence of Necessity* to be believed? Not more Evidence of *Truth*: For you confess the certain *Truth* of all the Bible, and that as fully manifest as your Additions. If it have more Evidence of *Necessity*, what is it? It is not because it is a *Divine Revelation*: For so you confess all the Bible to be? And do you pretend to a Tradition that saith, [You may be saved without most of the Bible, though it be of God, but not without fasting on *Frydays*, or on the Vigils of Saints-days, or other such Traditions?] But if you will make both the whole *Bible*, and *Tradition necessary to be*

B 2 *be-*

believed, it muſt be either Explicitely, or as you call it, *Implicitely:* If Explicitely, (that is, as each Point is particularly underſtood and believed,) then it's doubtful whether there be one Man in the World that is a Chriſtian, and can be ſaved? If *Implicitely,* that is, *Virtually* as it is in ſome General Propoſition, what is that *General?* Is it that *All that God revealeth is true?* Or that *All that the Spirit of Chriſt in his Apoſtles delivered to the Church as his word, is true.* Theſe we all agree in, if this will ſerve the turn? Is it that the Church is the *Miniſterial Keeper* of the Sacred Doctrine as delivered? This alſo we agree in. Or is it that *the Church de eventu ſhall never corrupt, alter, or loſe, this word, or any part of it?* If you mean it of every particular Church, we are agreed of the contrary. You confeſs that many Churches have fallen to Hereſie, and many Apoſtatized from the Faith: If you ſpeak of the *Univerſal Church,* we are agreed that the *Univerſal Church* ſhall never Apoſtatize ; for if Chriſt had no Church, he were no *Head* of it. And we are agreed that they ſhall never turn ſuch *true Hereticks,* as hold not truly *all the Eſſentials of Chriſtianity:* For ſuch alſo are *no Chriſtians* ; becauſe each Eſſential part is neceſſary to the *Eſſence.* But whether the *Univerſal Church,* much more the *Greater part,* may not make or receive ſome culpable alteration by Amiſſion, Omiſſion, or Commiſſion, we have reaſon to queſtion? We never heard any Proof that the Negative was neceſſary to Salvation, nor is it held by all your ſelves; and whether by any one man I cannot tell: For you take the Bible to be Gods Word, and your knowledge of the various Readings of the Hebrew and Greek Copies, and the multitude of Errours in the Vulgar Latine corrected by *P. Clem.* 8. and *Sixtus* 5. do ſatisfie all the World, that you hold that the

Uni-

Univerſal Church, or the major part, even your own, may culpably erre, or alter the very written Word of God. And who would then believe you, if you ſaid, [*But the Unwritten Word it cannot alter?*] It's true indeed, the *Eſſentials* conſidered, as Written or Unwritten, all the true Church, nor any one Chriſtian, while ſuch, cannot deny: But ſure, if many thouſand Errours may be found in that Book which you take your ſelves for the Word of God, and this through the fault or failing of ſuch as have had the keeping of it ; and *all Divine Revelations* are to be *believed*, and all the *Word of God is Divine Revelation*, it notoriouſly followeth, That your own Church hath not kept all that is *matter of Divine Faith* from alteration. So that though many of your Wranglers will not diſtinguiſh the *Eſſentials* of Chriſtianity (called Fundamentals) from the *Integrals* and *Accidentals*, (as if Chriſtianity were nothing, and had no determinate Eſſence,) yet this ſheweth, that you muſt do it whether you will or not ; or elſe you muſt confeſs that your Church may alter any thing, or every thing, as it hath done all theſe fore-mentioned : Which we will not confeſs of the Church Univerſal.

But, I ſuppoſe that we have not yet met with the Faith that you account neceſſary to ſalvation: *It is that the Pope of Rome, and a General Council, cannot erre, in delivering to us the Apoſtolical Doctrine to be believed.* And this is an implicite believing of all that is written in Scripture, and that is delivered orally from the Apoſtles. If ſo, words and names go very far with you as to mens ſalvation. Is this to believe a thouſand things which a man never knew or heard of? if he do but believe the Infallibility of your Church? What! Believe that which I never once thought of? But this is but *Implicite Faith?*

A

A cheating Name for *No-belief of those things*: For by *Implicite* here you can mean only *Virtual*, and that is no *Actual Belief* of that thing at all, but of something else, which would infer more were it known: Nay *Virtual* is too high a Name for it.

But will this serve the turn to salvation, to believe that *the Pope and his Council are Infallible*? What! though the same Person believe not in God the Father, Son, and Holy Ghost, nor any of the Articles of his Creed, no not a Life to come? If you say, Yea; Then will you call this Christianity, to believe in the Pope, and not in Christ? Or do you mean, that men may be saved without Christianity, but not without Popery? If so, why was not the Popes Name, rather than Christs, put into Baptism and the Creed, or at least with Christs?

But the insuperable difficulty is, How must I believe that the Pope hath this Infallibility? From Christ, or otherwise? If not from Christ, tell me which way, and why I must believe it? If from Christ, can I believe that the Pope hath Power from Christ, before I believe that there is a Christ, that hath such Power to give? And can I believe in Christ, and not believe that there is a God that sent him? Can I believe that Jesus is the Christ, and not believe that he is a Sacrifice for sin, or a Mediator between God and Man, and came to save his People from their sins? And can I believe this, and not believe that we are all sinners, and that sin deserveth that punishment which Christ came to save us from? Is not our Saviour, and our Sin and Misery relatives? as a Physician, or Medicine and a Disease? And can we believe that we have sin and desert of Punishment, without believing that God is our Governour, and gave us that Law which we broke, and which obligeth us to Punishment? Can

we

we believe in Christ, and not believe that he is God and Man, that he dyed, rose, and ascended into Heaven, and will judge us at last? and that he pardoneth sin, reneweth Souls by his Spirit, and will give us life hereafter? All these are included in believing in Christ, as Christ. And how must I believe that Christ hath given the Pope this Infallibility or Power? By any written word which granteth it? or by Oral Tradition? If by the written Word, then I must believe that that Word is true, before I can believe that the Pope is made Pope or Infallible by it? If by Oral Tradition, whose must that be? Then I must believe some bodies Oral Tradition as true and infallible, before I believe in the Pope at all. If it be the first Hearers of the Apostles, then either the Pope was one of those, or not. If *yea*, and he hath a Negative Voice in the credible report, then I must believe him as Infallible, before he is proved Infallible, in order to my believing that he is *Infallible*, which is a contradiction. If *Not*, Then I must believe the Infallibility of *other Hearers* of the Apostles, before I can believe the Pope's? And the Question will recur, How I shall know them to be Infallible? And who they were that were those Infallible Witnesses? Whether Pastors only, or the People? Whether of some one Church, or of all the Churches? And how I shall prove that they gave such a Testimony?

So that your pretense of a Necessity of receiving Gods Word, or the Christian Faith, from the Pope and his Council cometh too late: For it seemeth that we must believe it first, before it be possible to believe in the Pope and Council as authorised by Christ.

And if my Implicite Faith be the Belief of this Article, [*Any Church in all the world, yea, the greater part*

of

of all the Churches, may err in matters of Faith, or Apoſtatize, and only the Pope of Rome *and his Council cannot :*] What Proof, or whoſe Tradition doth this reſt upon?

Q. 9. Do not *Bellarmine, Coſterus*, and many of your Writers profeſs that the Scriptures contain all things ordinarily neceſſary to Salvation? Yea many Writers, that the Creed hath all that is abſolutely to be believed? Yea ſome, that it hath more than all? Yea abundance (Cited by *Fr. a Sancta Clara*) that the Belief in Chriſt is not neceſſary to all? And will you ſay then, that he that believeth Explicitely the *whole Bible* cannot be ſaved without believing alſo your pretended Traditions?

Q. 10. And do you not hereby, inſtead of the *light burden and eaſie yoak* of Chriſt, and his *Commands which are not grievous*, bring Chriſtians under a harder yoak than that which the *Jews* were not able to bear? When it ſeemed good to the Holy Ghoſt in the Apoſtles to impoſe but a few and neceſſary things, *Act.* 15. 28. And how large a Law is all the Bible, and all your Councils Decrees, and Oral Traditions, ſet together? Do all your Prieſts themſelves, or one of an hundred, underſtand them all, or know what they are?

Q. 11. While you pretend a Neceſſity of your numerous Ceremonies, (as Faſting on *Frydays*, and ſuch other named by you,) do you not lay a ſnare of perpetual Diviſion in the Churches? and do you not make as many inconſiſtent Churches, as there be Societies of Chriſtians that differ (and ſtill will differ) about any of thoſe Traditions or Ceremonies?

Q. 12. And do you not lay open your own Church, to the accuſation of *innovation, mutability*, and *corruption*, when it is not to be denyed, but in ſuch things as thoſe they have been mutable or innovated? Have you not

not long left the Custom of *adoring on the Lords-days without genuflexion*, though the first great General Council (*Nic. Can.* 20.) and the ancient Fathers commonly, made it a Tradition, and Practice of the whole Church? and it was Decreed to be so used by all? Abundance of such Instances may be given.

Q. 13. You do very injuriously to your own Sect and Cause, here to pretend Tradition as coming down from the Apostles, for such things as your own Doctors plead but your Churches later Institution for: It's fully proved by *Daleus de jejuniis*, that the Lent Fast was long but for a short time, before it came to fourty days: And it's an odd thing, if you will pretend Tradition from the Apostles, for the Holy-days, or the Vigil Fasts, of those Saints that were born many hundred years after the Apostles death?

We confess our Faith is not so big as yours? We have many score Texts of Scripture that promise Salvation to them that believe much less than the Bible it self containeth. Yet we profess our selves ready to believe as much more as you shall ever prove to us, to have been delivered by the Apostles, to the Church, to be believed.

II. And for the second, (that we *receive not our Faith the way that you do*; that is, from the *Authority of the Pope and Papists*, and from *your Tradition* :) We crave your consideration of these Questions.

1. When the Apostles (*and Disciples, Act.* 8.) were scattered, and preached the Gospel to many Nations, Were they not true Christians, and saved, that received the Gospel from any one of them, or from any Person whatsoever? If *Aquila* or *Priscilla* Converted a Sinner, such a one saved a Soul from Death, though *Peter* did it not; nor his Authority was known to such a one?

C   2. Do

(18)

2. Do you believe that if the *Roman* Bishop or Churches Revelation or Proposal were necessary to true Faith and to Salvation, that Christ would never have told Men so? Nor any of his Apostles have left it us on Record? When there were Heresies and Schismes so wofully troubling the Churches as we find in *Paul*'s Epistles to the *Cor. Gal. Col.* and in the *Rev.* 2. and 3. *ch.* should we never have found one word for this speedy way of decision, to appeal to the Church of *Rome*? Would *Paul* have rebuked them for saying, *I am of Cephas*, and made him but a *Minister by whom they believed*, without ever mentioning his Office and Dignity? would he never have told the Church of *Rome* of their Mistrisship and Infallibility above the rest? Would so necessary a Fundamental of Faith have been so much silenced?

3. Did the Apostles, Evangelists, or ancient Fathers, use to Convert Infidels by any such Method, and telling them that they must believe, first the Infallibility of the Bishop of *Rome* and his Clergie, and then believe the Gospel because he saith it is true? Had this been the old Method, would there not have been more Books necessary, and written, to prove this first Fundamental (the *Infallibility of the* Roman *Bishop and his Councils*) than to have proved the Gospel it self directly? Is it not a wonder that we should have such Volumes as *Eusebius* his *Præparatio. & Demonstratio Evangel.* and so many written by those before and after him, to prove the *Gospel*, and none of them hit on this Method; nor write at large to make it good? The Churches Authority and Unity, is ordinarily pleaded against *Heresies and Schismes*, but who ever Converted *Infidels* by the Authority of the Papal Church, either proved or asserted as the necessary *Medium* of Faith?

4. Do

4. Do you not confess that all other Churches may erre besides the *Roman*? And their plea of Tradition you account invalid: Your Book called [*Considerations on the Council of Trent*, by *R. H.*] *p.* 40. faith, [" *All Con-*
" *ciliary Definitions are not only Declarations and Testifi-*
" *cations of such Apostolical Traditions as were left by them*
" *evident and conspicuous in all Christian Churches Planted*
" *by them; but are many times Determinations of Points*
" *deduced from, and necessary consequents to, such clear Tradi-*
" *tionals, whether written or unwritten.* 2. *If the Acts*
" *of General Councils were only such Declarations of Apo-*
" *stolical Tradition, yet it is possible that some particular*
" *Church, may in time, depart from such a Tradition en-*
" *trusted to them; else how can any Church become Hereti-*
" *cal against any such Tradition?*]

Do you not at this day accuse the *Greek Church*, the *Muscovites*, the *Armenians*, the *Jacobites*, *Syrians*, *Coptics*, *Abassines*, the *Protestants*, &c. as having departed from, or corrupted the first Tradition? And how *small a* part of the *Universality* of Christians are the *Papists*? And if the *greater* part of Christians may so forsake the Apostolical Tradition, why may not the Pope of *Rome* and his Council? How shall we be sure of their exemption from such danger? You tell us over and over of our receiving this and that from our Fathers and Grand-Fathers? And is that a certain Proof that it is Apostolical? Why is it not so then with all the rest, the *Abassines*, the *Armenians*, &c. and the Majority of Christians? But of this I have spoken in the former Treatise.

5. And there I have desired you to tell us, whether your *Grandfather*, or his *Priest*, was *Infallible*? If yea, how came he by it more than *all those Churches*? If not, do you not delude your Relations, by drawing them to build their

their Faith on a fallible man, or upon nothing? Your Relations were not at the Council of *Trent*, or *Florence*, or *Laterane*: How shall they be sure what the Pope and Council agreed on? What Foundation, but the words of your Priest or Grandfather, have you for your assurance? May not one of your Priests lye as well as all the *Greek*, *Abassine*, &c. Churches? When Pope *Cælestine* himself falsly urged the *Nicene* Council for Appeals to *Rome*, contrary to *Augustine* and the *Carthage* Council? Either tell your Readers plainly, that it's *you*, and such *as you*, that are the *Infallible Foundation* of their Faith; or bid them stay, and not go your way, till they are certain what the Pope and his Council say; and that he is a true Pope, and it a true Council, and that they are more Infallible than the major part of Christians. And our Faith can be no stronger than the weakest necessary *medium* of it, from whence it must arise.

6. I have said so much of this in a small Book, called, [*The certainty of Christianity without Popery*,] which I intreat you impartially to peruse; where I have also shewed the utter uncertainty that Popery would reduce our Christianity to; that I will now only tell you, that after your talk of Tradition, and Church, and Fathers, and Grandfathers, if we had not much more *testimony of Tradition* for our Religion than you have for Popery, we should think our Faith were very lame. Compare ours with yours: 1. Yours is *A pretended Authoritative determination*, which rests upon a supposed *Inspiration* of some Persons, by virtue of a special Priviledge peculiar to themselves. 2. It is the Tradition of the *minor part* of Christians against the *major*. 3. It rests on the pretended *Infallibility* of a *Pope*, *which great General Councils* have said may be a *Heretick*, and have deposed divers

as

as Hereticks, and worſe: And upon the Infallibility of *General Councils*, which by Popes and other Councils are pronounced fallible, unleſs confirmed by a Pope (who may be a Heretick.) 4. It reſts upon a Foundation (*viz.* the Popes Divine Right of Primacy and Infallibility) which is expreſly denied by two of the firſt four great General Councils, approved to this day; *viz.* that of *Calcedon* reciting the ſenſe of that of *Conſtantinople* againſt the ſaid Divine right, affirming, that the *Popes Primacy was given him by the Fathers, becauſe* Rome *was the Imperial Seat*. 5. It reſts upon an Authority (of Popes and General Councils,) which being at firſt but the *Clergie* of *one Empire*, hath thence claimed the ſame Power over *all the Chriſtian World*, which they had got in the Dominions of *one Prince*. 6. It reſts on a Claim downright contradictory to it ſelf, as aforeſaid, *viz.* That we muſt believe that the Pope hath this Power and Infallibility given him and his Councils, by Chriſt and his Goſpel, before we can believe that there is a Chriſt and a Goſpel authorized and true.

Now our Tradition is this: For all the *Eſſentials* of our Religion, the Sacramental Covenant, and the three expoſitory *Symbols,* we have the currant Tradition both of the Papiſts and all the reſt of the Chriſtian World: Yea, that *every Book* that we call Canonical is the true Word of God, not only the Papiſts but almoſt all the Chriſtian World confeſs: And, *de facto*, that theſe *Books* came down from the Apoſtles, at leaſt that the Goſpel was preached by them, we have the Teſtimony alſo of Enemies and Perſecutors. And are not all theſe more than the Teſtimony of one *Sect* alone? 2. And in this we have as much to confirm us as you have, of the *wiſdom, piety, care of the Church to preſerve* the Goſpel, and

much

much more too ; for we have the *Piety* of *all the Churches* to plead, and not *your Sect alone* : And we undertake to prove such a *moral Infallibility* as is also *Natural*, *viz.* That Mans *Nature* and *Interests* supposed, it is no more possible for so many Persons and Nations of cross Interests to have agreed in their Testimony for the Gospel, than for all the contentious Lawyers in the Land to have agreed falsly to inform us, that our Statutes were made by such Kings and Parliaments. But a domineering Faction alone might easilier have deceived men.

3. Yea, even as to *Christs Promise*, we can better prove that the *Universal Church*, or *Body of Christians*, shall *never lose the Faith*, than you can prove it of *Rome alone*, or the *Papal Sect*. *Bellarmine* himself dare not say, that *Rome* shall not cease to be the seat of the *Papacy*, or shall not be utterly destroyed. And then how can there be a *Bishop of Rome*, when there is no *Rome*? But you'll say, that if he dwell at *Avignion*, he may be *called Bishop of Rome*? But if he be *called so* when *he is not so*, at least when there is *no Rome*, or *no Christian Church there*, sure a *false Name* is not an Essential part of our Religion. If you say, that at *Avignion*, or *Ravenna*, or *Vienna*, he may be S. *Peter*'s Successor, and so the Universal Monarch still. I answer, Then it seems that the Council of *Calcedon*, as afore-cited, was in the right, (that *Romes Priviledge was given by the Fathers, because it was the Imperial Seat* :) And so that the Pope is not S. *Peter*'s Successor, *eo nomine*, because *he is Bishop of Rome*. But if the Bishop of *Avignion*, or *Vienna*, might become S. *Peter*'s Successor (who never was Bishop there,) how shall we know that the Bishop of *Rome* is his Successor *now*? We have hitherto had no better means to prove it, and deceive the World, than by saying that S. *Peter* dyed Bishop

of

of *Rome*, where the Pope is Bishop: But S. *Peter* dyed not Bishop of *Avignion*. If the *Place* prove not the *Succession*, tell us, if you can, what doth? Is it the *Election*? By whom? Who are those men that have the Power of chusing S. *Peter* a Successor? You know, I suppose, that the Pope hath been chosen, 1. Sometime by the People, (witness the blood-shed at the choice of *Damasus* in the Church:) 2. Sometime by the People, and the Neighbour Ordaining Bishops: 3. Sometime by a Synod: 4. Sometime by the Emperours: 5. And lastly, by the *Roman* Cardinals. If any of these may chuse, then we may have four or five lawful Popes, chosen four or five several ways, at once. If only one of these have the Power, S. *Peter* had no Successors under all the other Elections. So that the Claim will fall rather to *Antioch* than to *Avignion*, or any other Town, because they say it was S. *Peter's* first Bishoprick, from which he removed for a greater. If you are driven with poor Mr. *Johnson*, alias, *Terret*, to say, that *Any way will serve which serveth for the truth of an Election of Princes, &c.* then still we may have four Popes at least. I doubt you must be forced to say as some, that it is the *acceptance of the Universal Church*, which must prove who is the *Universal Monarch*. 1. But some must be *Electors*, before it comes to acceptance. And who hath the Power of *Electing*? And 2. what if now the major part of the Church should prefer the Bishop of *Constantinople*? I hope you are not so ignorant of Cosmography as not to know that the *Greek* Church when they first preferred the Bishop of *Const.* was far greater than the *Latine*. 3. And I suppose you know that it is not near half the Christian World that now accepteth of the Pope as their Governour. 4. And I pray you do but get the Pope to suspend his claim till *the Church Universal*

verſal accept him, and we ſhall not be troubled with him: For how ſhall they ſignifie their acceptance? If in a General Council, you know how they of *Conſtance, Baſil,* and *Piſa,* are reviled by the Pope and thoſe that now go for your Church, for pretending to a power to depoſe and chuſe Popes; and how *Eugenius* the fourth prevailed againſt ſuch a Depoſition. And if theſe Councils were not your Univerſal Church repreſentative, where ſhall we think to find it?

In ſum, we have the *Tradition* of a Church as *big as three of the* Roman *for all our Religion*; and of *all the* Roman *Church* it ſelf; beſides the Confeſſion of the *Enemies* of the Church, Pagans, Infidels, Mahometans, Jews, and Hereticks; we have not one word that's part of our Religion, which your ſelves confeſs not to be true: We believe that the *Faith of the Univerſal Church ſhall never fail,* nor the Gates of Hell prevail againſt it: And ſo you ſee that we may far better tell how Infallibly we have received our Religion from our Forefathers, than you can do of yours: But we believe not that this Univerſal Church hath any *Head* but *Chriſt*; no Humane Vicarious Monarch or Governour of all the World: We believe that Men muſt Believe in Chriſt before they can know that the Pope is his Vicar, if it had been true: We know, as ſure as Hiſtory can tell us, that the Pope's firſt Primacy, and the reſt of the Patriarchates were but the Humane Ordinances of the Clergie of one Empire, and not of the whole Chriſtian World. And we know not (nor you) but *Rome* and its Church and Biſhop, may yet all ceaſe together.

But you make me moſt admire at you, that (in this Book alſo) you tell your Relations, and other Readers, of the *uncertainty of notice by Books* in Compariſon of

Con-

converse and *talk* with those of your *present Party*; yea that your *own Religion* is not to be known by *Books*, as being lyable to be misunderstood, so well as by talking with Papists, and asking them what is their Faith or Religion. Sir, I judge by your Stile that you are a man of zeal and conscience in your way, and therefore that you write not this fraudulently against your conscience. Sure then you must needs be a man of more than ordinary ignorance, that can believe what you say. 1. Is it your *Objective* or your *Subjective* Faith that we are disputing of? If it be not the *Rule* and *Object* of your Faith, every man indeed may tell us what *he believeth himself*, but no man can tell us what *another* believeth. And then you have as many Religions as men; for every man hath one of his own, and no two men in the world know and believe just all the same things, neither more nor less: And what shall those of us think of your Religion then, who find that one of you affirmeth what another denyeth? For instance, A worthy Person of your Religion affirmed to me, that notwithstanding the Fifth Commandment [*Honour thy Father and Mother*,] a Mother hath not any Governing Power over a *Child*, nor the *Child* oweth any obedience to the Mother, during the Fathers life, because it were confusion were there more Governours in a House than one, though subordinate one to the other. Is this your common Judgment? May I say therefore that this is other mens belief? You know that when we aliedge the sayings of your most Learned Writers, we are ordinarily told, that it is not the judgment of particular Doctors, but of the Church in Councils, which we must call your Churches Judgment. You undertake not to justifie any more. And if I talk with

D any

any of my Neighbours and ask him what he believeth, have I any more than a single Doctors opinion? Is his Answer, the Faith of your Church? But would you have any one past seven years old believe you, that *writing* is of no more use to Memory for conservation of Antiquities? when God would not trust his *Ten Commandments* to the Peoples *Memories*, but would write them in Stone, and put them in the Arke, (which you have so little skill in Antiquity as to say here was the *first writing*: Sure if you will read your Jesuite *Euseb. Nirembergius de Antiqu. scripturæ* you will not say that your Grand-Father taught you truly that Opinion as the Tradition of the Church.) Why do *you write* to your own Relations, if writing be so un-intelligible? Could the *Bible* have been kept as well in Memory as by *Writings*? Why were the Gospels written then? Do you go to *Tradition*, or to *Books*, to decide any Controversie now of the various readings? Did Pope *Clem.* 8. and *Sixtus* 5. reform the vulgar *Latine* by *Memory* or by *Books*? Pope *Pius*'s *Trent* Oath sweareth Men to Interpret Scripture according to the consent of the Fathers: Do any of your Doctors know how that is by *Memory and Oral Tradition*, or by *Books*? Did *Possevine*, and *Sixtus Senensis*, and such others, Correct Books by Oral Tradition, or by Books? Did *Celestine* and the *Carthage* Council debate the Case of the *Nicene* Canon (a narrow Instance which Memory might have served for) out of Mens *Memories*, or out of *written Records*? Why doth *Turrian* bring us out new Forged Canons, and why do the Copies of many Councils differ in the recital of Canons, if Memory and Universal un-written Tradition can reconcile the difference? Was the *Athenian* Philosophy propagated and preserved better by Memory, or by Books? Why is

not

not the Stoicks, and Epicureans, and others, as fully known now as *Aristotles* and *Plato's*, if Memory without Books could have done? Have you as full notice now of the Acts of *James, John, Matthew, Thomas, Bartholomew, &c.* without Book, as you have of *Paul's* by the Book? Is memory sufficient to have preserved to us the Statutes of the Land, without Books and Records? Yea, or the Common-Law without any Records or Book Cases? Why are all your Councils written? and all the Decretals? to say nothing of the Civil *Roman* Laws, Institutes, Pandects, and Digests. Can you decide the Controversies about the Decretals, published by *Isidore Mercator*, by Tradition? What are all your Libraries for at the *Vatican, Florence, Paris*, and in each Learned Mans House, if Books be so useless and unintelligible? If one of your Relations ask you, what is in the Council of *Trent, Florence, Laterane*, and so upward, can you tell him fully without Book by Tradition? And are not these Councils your very Religion? Doth every Papist Neighbour carry them all in his brain, more certainly than in Books? Or could your Grandfather and Grandmother have told us more certainly what is in them, than *Crab, Syrius, Binius, Baronius, Justellus, Albaspinæus, Petavius, Sirmondus, &c.* could do? Or is all left uncertain because it is written?

Through Gods Mercy our Essentials, and somewhat more, are delivered certainly down to us by two hands, by Oral and Practical Tradition, and by the Scripture, because they lye in a narrow room. But yet if you had the front to tell the World, that your immutable Church hath never changed the Creed it self; we could not believe you, because Books contradict you. Tradition from your Great Grandfather cannot assure us that [*Filioq;*] was

was in the Creed from the days of the Apoſtles: Nor that [*the Holy Catholick Church, the Communion of Saints,*] and the other words mentioned in *Voſſius*, and *Uſher de Sym'olis*, were in ſo long: Nor that the *Greeks* added no words to their Creed at *Nice*, nor afterward at *Conſtantinople*, in General Councils; nor that all S. *Hilaries* outcry againſt Creeds was in vain. Nor can Tradition without Book yet aſſure us, what were the very words of the Creed uſed commonly by the *Greeks*, immediately before the *Nicene* Council; nor who wrote that aſcribed to *Athanaſius*: Nor among the various *Formula's* of that called the Apoſtles, found, as aforeſaid, in *Ireneus*, *Tertullian*, *Epiphanius*, *Ruffinus*, *&c.* which of them was in conſtant uſe; or whether liberty of ſuch alteration of words was not then uſed.

And no Unwritten Report of your Grandfather can aſſure us, that your Maſs-Book or Liturgy was the ſame in the Apoſtles days as it is now; nor that it was for 600 years the ſame in all the Churches of one Empire; and that every Biſhop had not power to uſe what Liturgy he pleaſed, in his own City or *Parochia*: Nor can your Tradition aſſure us, that what the Father and Grandfather uſed, was uſed from the Apoſtles, when the Church of *Neocæſarea* clamoured at S. *Baſil* for his ſingularity and innovations, and S. *Baſil* retorts on them, that they at *Neocæſarea* had ſcarce left any thing unchanged: I hope this is not the leſs credible becauſe *Baſil* hath *written* it.

At leaſt, I pray hereafter give over your ill practice of leading ſimple Readers into a Wood of *Church-Hiſtory*, to loſe them and the Queſtion there among a multitude of Citations of old Books, when you know not what elſe to ſay (as *William Johnſon* did,)

becauſe

becaufe there the ignorant know nothing themfelves, but may as well believe the Affirmer as the Denyer; and at leaft the diverfion to voluminous Controverfies about particular mens words may hide your Errours. Do not refolve all the Controverfie, yea the Faith of your Followers, into a multitude of *Books* of *Councils* and *Fathers* which they never faw. And do not take fo much care to corrupt and alter Books, for your intereft, as inftances and your *Indices Expurg.* tell us you have done. Refolve without Book the Controverfie about your great *Laterane* Council, whether Dr. *Taylor*, Dr. *Pierfon*, Dr. *Gunning*, (and Bifhop *Coufins* lately) that fay *Innocent.* 3. made and publifhed the Canons, and the Council did not confent to them, be in the right, or rather they that anfwered Dr. *Pierfon* and Dr. *Gunning*, and indeed your Church, which holds the contrary (which Mr. *Dodwell* feemeth to me lately to have fully proved, in his Book about tolerating Papifts.)

Nay why may we not expect that you lay by your Book Catechifms, your Office Books, your Controverfie Books, and teach your People all without Book?

But by this Counfel to your Relations, you fully fhew that you would have them to have no certainty at all, either what Chriftianity is, or what Popery is. For they fhall never fpeak with the *Univerfal Church*, or with a *General Council*, while they live; And all their Neighbours, to whom you fend them, are fallible Perfons. I fuppofe you one of the chief of them, and alas, how fallible you are, you have in two Writings grofly fhewed.

Having faid thus much, more, to fhew that your Foundation is Sand, who fend us from *Books* to our Grandfathers, as infallible; and that this is no better a ground

than

than the *Abaſſines*, *Greeks*, and others, may build on as well as you; and that we our selves have a far surer and Universal Tradition than the Papacy hath, and have your own consent to every word of our Objective Religion, I now proceed to consider of your Character of Parties.

CHAP. II.

YOU describe to us four supposed Parties. I. The *Puritan*. II. The *Prelatical Proteſtant*, (whom your *Fitz-Simmons* calleth, The *Formaliſt*.) III. The *Papiſt*, as you suppose us *falſly to deſcribe him*. IV. The *Papiſt*, as you suppose him *truly deſcribed*, whom you call *The Apoſtolical Chriſtian*. In all which you shew that you are far from Infallibility, and a man unfit for your Relations to trust in so great a Case.

I. I confess you give the *Puritan* a very laudable description, in comparison of the *Prelatiſt Proteſtant*, and the *feigned Papiſt*. And you tell us, that you were once a Puritan your self, and you own still that which you describe as *Puritaniſm*, only adding *Popery* to it, which you think it wants. I confess you speak incomparably more honourably and charitably of *Puritans*, than some malicious interessed Persons, of their own Protestant Profession will do. But,

1. You deal not informingly, in your *deſcribing* a *Puritan*, before you *diſtinguiſh* that ambiguous ill-made word. It hath three common acceptions among us at least.

First, The *ancienteſt*, as it signifieth the old or later
Catharists,

Catharists, who held that they *were perfect* (if they are not belyed:) And none come nearer these than the Papists and Quakers, certainly *Protestants* are far from it.

Secondly, the *old Non-conformists* had the name of *Puritanes* put on them, by those that were against them: For what reason, I leave them to answer to God.

Thirdly, and because these *Non-conformists* lived *strictly*, and were for much preaching, and praying, and holy conference, and spending the Lords-day in holy Exercises, and serious diligence in working out our Salvation, and were sharp against drunkenness, swearing, and such other sins, therefore the *vulgar Rabble* of vicious ones, that durst not rail at Piety under the name of Piety, took the advantage of the Bishops displeasure at the Non-conformists, and of the name *Puritane*, and put that name upon all Christians among them, that were *notably serious in practical Godliness*, perswading themselves that they were all but *Hypocrites*: And so the name among the *vulgar Rabble* grew common to *godly Conformists and Non-conformists*: And as if *loquendum cum vulgo* had been a Law, by this means the Devil did more hurt both to *godliness* (rendring it among the vulgar to be but odious Hypocrisie and Singularity) and to *Episcopacy* (making Multitudes that disliked the wickedness of the Rabble, to think that all this came from the Bishops,) and it did more to advance and honour the *Non-conformists*, (because the name was formerly *theirs* as such) than by any one thing that I remember in all my younger days. This the godly Conformists grievously complained of, (as Bishop *Downame* in his *Spittle Sermon*, called *Abrahams Tryal*, and Mr. *Robert Bolton*, who saith, that he *believeth that never poor persecuted word passed through the Mouths of wicked Men with more bitter scorn, since Ma-*
lice

lice firſt entred into the Heart of Man:] Really the permitting of the common Rabble of all the debauched Sinners of the Land to make ſerious godlineſs a common ſcorn under the name of Puritaniſme, had as great a hand as any thing I know in all our Confuſions.

Fourthly, and it added Fuel to the Fire when ſome brought up a fourth fence of the Word (ſome ſay, *Mar. Ant. de Dom. Spalatenſis* was the inventor of it,) and that was *Doctrinal Puritanes*, by which name they underſtood thoſe by ſome called *Calviniſts*, by others *Anti-Arminians*, who held the Doctrine of your Dominicans, or of the Janſeniſts.

Now who can well tell which of theſe ſorts of Puritanes you *were*, and *talk of*, while you Characterize the *ſecond ſort*, as well as the *firſt*, and yet diſtinguiſh them from *Prelatick Proteſtants*?

2. But which ever it is, obſerve here that you own the *Puritanes Religion* ſtill, and ſay, [*I have not ſo much left Puritaniſm, as Prelaticks call it, as added that to it wherein I found it come ſhort of the holy Apoſtles Doctrine and Inſtitutions,*] *p.* 1. And when you have deſcribed the Puritane as one ſeriouſly conſcionable and regardful of his Salvation, (at large) you add, [*If this be to be a Puritane, would to God all the World were Puritanes! I am ſo far from being Converted from thus much of a Puritane, that I moſt heartily wiſh I could Convert all the World to it.*]

3. But yet your deſcription of him is ſo very falſe, that I may conclude when you turned, as you think, from being a meer Puritane to be a Papiſt, you never knew what a *Puritane is*, nor indeed ever were a *Puritan* your ſelf, unleſs you take the word as fitted to your ſelf, and ſuch as you.

If

If you had meant by a *Puritane* a meer *Non-conformist* as such, you would not so laudably have described the work of God upon his Soul and Life as you have done: For if most Non-conformists be such, yet so are many others as well as they. And it's easie to see what a deceitful course it is to take up a name of many significations, and such as signifieth no different Religion at all, as to any one Article of Faith, nor any more difference in, or about Religion, than such as is among most Christian Churches; and much less than is among your selves.

Besides that the plainer name of a *Non-conformist* is of no determinate nor certain signification, save only in general to notifie one that Conformeth not to all that is imposed on him; but *what that is*, the *name* doth not signifie.

A *Non-conformist* in *Scotland* is one thing, in *England* another thing, as the Impositions are different. Non-conformity twenty years ago, or fourty years, was one thing. Non-conformity since 1662. is quite another thing. And Non-conformists differ among themselves: If twenty things be imposed as necessary to the Ministry, he is a Non-conformist who consenteth but to nineteen of them; and so is he that consenteth but to eighteen, or to seventeen, or to sixteen, and so on, as well as he that consenteth to none of them. And that there is so much difference among them is no wonder to them, nor any considerate Man; for they hold Christian Love and Communion with those that agree with them in the foresaid common Principles and Practice of Christianity, (as far as they require not them to sin:) And they are not of a different Religion from every one that *fasteth not on Fridays*, or *Saints Vigils*, &c. as you seem to be, nor

E   from

from every one that doth so ; nor from every one that thinketh not in every thing as they think, or that prayeth in other words than they ; for no two Men in the World should on such Terms be of one Religion: They believe *Socrates* and *Sozomen*, who tell us of the great diversity of Rites and Orders in the ancient Churches, which all consisted with the same Religion, Faith, and Love. They abhor the Principle of hating, persecuting, yea and separating from one another for such differences as will unavoidably adhere to the imperfect condition of Christians here on Earth.

At this time in *England* a considerable part (if not the far greatest) of the *silenced Ministers* are for the *Primitive Episcopacy*, and *some Liturgie*, as you may see in their offer of A. Bishop *Usher*'s *Reduction* to the King, and their desires of a *reformed Liturgie*. Among the *old Non-conformists*, there were divers degrees : such as Dr. *Regnolds*, Mr. *Perkins*, Dr. *Humfrey*, *Paul Bayn*, &c. did yield to more than some others could do. How can you tell then by the name of a *Puritane*, what to charge any single Person with?

But it seemeth you take their *Non-conformity in General*, and their *temper of mind and life together*. But then you greatly wrong them, and seem not at all to know what their Religion is.

There are two things which you say they mistake in : 1. Their Doctrine of *Imputed Righteousness, and the Covenant, and not solicitously endeavouring after the acquisition of Virtue*, because they trust to the *Imputed Righteousness*;] your words are too large to recite: You partly here unworthily injure them by ascribing to them the very *opinions* and *words* of the *Antinomians*, whom they have better confuted than ever you did. And as to their Doctrine

ctrine of *Imputed Righteousness*, even *Bellarmine* in one sense owneth it: And whether our sense be found I provoke you to try particularly by your perusal of my own Writings on that Subject, especially a late *Treatise* of [*Justifying Righteousness* and Imputation,] and a Treatise called [*Catholick Theologie*:] In which if there be nothing which you *dare* or *can* confute, judge whether your meer derision of [*Imputative Righteousness*] be not delusory: If you dare say, that *you trust not to Christs Sacrifice, and meritorious perfect righteousness*, as procuring you *pardon and life*, (*Jus ad Impunitatem & Regnum Cælorum*,) enjoy your self-confidence while you can. But if you say in this *as we*, then make publick Confession of the injury of your reproach of such *Imputed Righteousness*, as you trust your salvation upon your self.

I imagine you will say, that *my judgment* is no certain signification of the judgment of the Puritans; for I am *singular*, and therefore what I say in these Books is no proof of the sense of the Non-conforming Puritans. But, 1. *my* judgment of their sense is as good as *yours*. 2. Do you know of any one Nonconformist that hath published any dissent to what I have written? (Dr. *Tully* was a *Conformist*.) 3. You profess (before) to borrow the name [*Puritan*] from the *Prelatists*. And I have this to say for my Authority in declaring the sense of Puritans, that one or more (whose *genius* is of kin to the *Roman*, but far *less mild* than *yours*) who are Prelatical or super-Prelatical, have about 17 years ago (being Masters of that Language) branded me with the Name of [*Purus putus Puritanus, & qui totum Puritanismum totus spirat.*] (The *Pseudo-Tilenus* hath just the same stile as the late *Unmasker of the Presbyterians*, who revileth modest, judicious, pious, and peaceable *J. Corbet*, and in the most ingenious strain of

wrath

wrath and malice doth valiantly militate againſt *Love*.) Therefore Prelatiſts being Judges, I may as credibly as another tell you what is the *Puritan Judgment*.

2. Your ſecond accuſation of the Puritan is, that [*He begins to quarrel with all external Worſhip and Ceremonies.*] But this is alſo ſpoken ignorantly and untruly: You before miſtook the *Antinomian* for the *Puritan*, and here you ſeem to take the *Separatiſt* for the *Puritan*. Read the Reformed Liturgy, and other Papers offered at the *Savoy* to the Biſhops, and you may ſee that though they are not for *ſilencing*, *excommunicating*, and *damning men* for a *Ceremony*, nor for making as many Religions, as there are differences about Ceremonies, yet they are for doing all things to edification, decently and in order; and for *external* as well as *internal* Worſhip of God: As knowing that the *Body* is his, and made to Worſhip him as well as the *Soul*, and therefore ſhould fall down and *kneel* before him, and reverently and holily behave it ſelf in his Service.

You ſay, p. 5. "[*He is much confirmed in this his imagi-*
"*nation, by conſidering the open profaneneſs, and little*
"*ſenſe of God, he obſerveth generally in zealous Confor-*
"*miſts. And on the other ſide he taketh notice of his Bre-*
"*thren the Non-conformiſts, that they are generally free*
"*from open and ſcandalous ſins, and at leaſt ſigh and breath*
"*after interior ſpirit and devotion, which certainly muſt*
"*be that muſt give us a title to Heaven, rather than a few*
"*Cringes, and exterior Verbal Devotions, which any one*
"*though never ſo prophane may eaſily exerciſe.*]

1. But do you not here and in your former deſcription quite contradict your ſelf, when you charge them as neglecting *inherent righteouſneſs*?

2. We are not ſo fooliſh as not to know, that the unreverent

reverent hypocritical abuse of Gods external Worship, by others whosoever, will not excuse us for neglecting it. Of the Conformists we must speak anon.

3. By the way I would you could impartially consider, if the Puritans be so good men, as you fairly confess them to be, what the reason is that Papists generally are far more fiery against them than against those whom you speak so meanly of as *Prelatical Protestants*? Remember how your Writer after the *London* Fire, answered by Dr. *Lloid*, did flatter these as more suitable to the Papists *genius* in comparison of the Puritans: And the *Unmasker* against *J. Corbet* will tell you out of *Watson* (an honourable Witness hanged for Treason in *Cobham*'s, &c. Conspiracy) how bad the Puritans are, (comparing them with the Jesuites:) And if your Laws took place in *England*, what abundance of these Puritans would you make Bonfires of? yea your own Relations were not like to scape you. They have told me to my face, how quickly they would otherwise silence me than the Prelates do, if I were in their power. And the Decrees *De Hæreticis comburendis & exterminandis* more fully tell it us. Yea, whence is it, that most certain experience proveth it, that by how much the nearer any Protestants genius is to the Papists, by so much the more *bloody, cruel, malicious,* or *slanderous* and *unmerciful* he is to the *Puritanes*?

You'll say for both, that it is because the *Puritans are most against them, and Interest ruleth the world.* But I answer, 1. God's Interest is highest with every true Christian: 2. I confess it's true, that Puritans are most against Popery: But truly as far as I have been acquainted with them, they are not most against your *Persons*, nor would have any injustice or cruelty exercised against you: But the fear of your *Faggots*, or *Powder-Plots*, and such

such *Massacres* as were in *France*, (of Thirty Thousand, or Forty Thousand;) or in *Ireland*, (of Two Hundred Thousand,) hath made them think your *Power* inconsistent with their safety: 3. And you must remember that the *Positive Additions* of the Church of *Rome* are in the Judgment of the Puritans very great sins: But you have truly no charge against the Puritans, for any one Article of their Religion; but only for *not receiving*, and for *protesting against your Additions*.

4. But I perceive, *p.* 5. your Instances of their defectiveness are, that they are not for ["*fasting days, particular Garments for Priests, set Forms, Christmas-day, Good-Friday, Ascension, Whitsuntide,* &c. *which they take for meer Humane inventions and Will-worship; Because they think that the New Testament was written to instruct us Christians in the whold Body of Gospel-worship, &c.*

But you are best prove this only by telling us that you know some persons of that mind: And when you have done, I will demand your Proof that those Persons are *no more* than Puritans: They have oft told you that their judgment is, that for all that substance of God's Worship which is of Universal necessity to the Church, and is of Divine Institution, the holy Scripture is a sufficient Rule: But that very many Circumstances and outward Acts have in Scripture but a General Law (that they be all done to edification, decently, orderly, in Concord, *&c.*) and it is left to Humane Prudence to order them by such Rules: We condemn no one that useth holy Fasts or Feasts, but think them needful: We judge not those that celebrate the Memorial of God's great Mercies to his Church, by giving him thanks for the holy Life and Doctrine of his Eminent Saints, *&c.* But will you plainly have our judgment? We

We think Saint *Paul* was in the right that taught the Church of *Rome* it self, both the *Rulers* and the Flocks, that they muſt neither *judge* nor *deſpiſe* each other for differences about Meats and Days, but *receive each other* (to Communion notwithſtanding ſuch differences) as *Chriſt received us*, Rom. 14. and 15. And we will not believe your Grand-Father, nor Great-Grand-Father, if they told us that the Apoſtles by Tradition did inſtitute Holy-days, and Vigils for St. *Tecla*, or St. *Bridgit*, or St. *Thomas Becket*, or any that were not born till they were dead: And any one *Day* or *Order* which you truly prove to us that the *Apoſtles* by Tradition ordained for the *Univerſal Church*, we profeſs our ſelves ready and reſolved to obey.

But if you plead not *Tradition* for any of *theſe things*, but the *Churches Commands*, (as you muſt do, or be ſingular, or aſhamed;) here you come to the quick of our difference: 1. We know not of any *Univerſal Vicarious Law-giver* under Chriſt that hath any power to make Laws to the Univerſal Church throughout the World: and we dare not own any ſuch *Uſurper* left we be guilty of Treaſon againſt the only Head of the whole Church.

2. We know not of any power that the chief Biſhop in the *Roman* Empire hath over other Empires, Kingdomes, or Churches.

3. But to our own *true Paſtors* which are ſet over us according to Chriſt's order and his Apoſtles recorded in Scripture, we Puritanes will ſubmit in all ſuch Circumſtantials, as aforeſaid, which are left to their prudent determination, not putting us on any ſin.

But, 4. We deteſt making ſuch things as you here name to be taken for the Characters of *diſtinct Religions*, or *diſtinct Churches*, as if we might not with Love, Peace, and Chriſtian Communion, differ about a Garment, a

Holy-

Holy-day, Fast, or Vigil. Thus far then you seem not to know what a meer Puritan is.

II. But, Sir, I have much more than all these little things against your Description of a Puritane: I plainly perceive in your greatest praises of him, that you know not what his very Religion it self is; or else you would never describe him as only taken up with *fears and cares, and good desires to be better*, having yet *greedy desires of the things of the world*, without any mention of the *Love of God above all*, and of his *Neighbour*, and a *holy and heavenly Mind and Life*, with *self-denyal, mortification* of the *Flesh*, &c.

Either you judge of a *Puritane* by what you were *your self*, or by what your *acquaintance* were, or by what they *commommonly profess* to be their Religion.

For the first you have no reason: It followeth not that *they* have no better a Religion, because *you* had no better.

For the second you had no reason: For it's ten to one you knew not the hearts of your acquaintance, so well as to be able to know that they had not the *Love of God, &c*. And if you were so unhappy in your acquaintance, what's that to other Men?

Thirdly, Therefore as you look that your own Religion should be described, not as we find it in this or that man, but as your Church professeth it, so do we: And I have told you before what our Religion is. I have the more boldness in speaking the sense of others, as I said, both because I am as aforesaid stigmatized for a *total Puritan*, and because the generality of all of them of my acquaintance as far as I can discern are of this mind.

A *Puritan* then, as the Word is commonly taken by the Rabble, is a *serious Christian Protestant, who truly believeth and practiseth what he doth profess*; and doth not mortifie

that

that Profeſſion which ſhould help to mortifie his Sin: His Religion is, to be underſtandingly and ſincerely devoted in the Sacramental Covenant to God the Father, Son, and Holy Ghoſt; renouncing the Vanities of the World, the Luſts of the Fleſh, and the Deluſions of the Devil: He believeth that all that truly conſent to this Covenant, have a right, and part, in, and to, the Love of God the Father, the Grace of the Son, and the Communion of the Holy Ghoſt; and that he that hath the Son hath Life, Pardon, Adoption, Juſtification, and Right to Life Eternal; and that this Right is continued, he performing his Covenant, and continuing in that Faith which worketh by Love, and not living impenitently in ſin, but ſincerely obeying God his Father, Saviour, and Sanctifier: He taketh the *fear* of Gods Juſtice, and godly Sorrow, to be but the lower ſteps of Holineſs; but that the Kingdom of God is (not Meats and Days, but) Righteouſneſs, Peace, and Joy in the Holy Ghoſt; and that the Spirit of Chriſt, without which none are his, is not the Spirit of Bondage, but of Power, Love, and a ſound Mind; even a Spirit of holy LIFE, LIGHT, and LOVE, which are the Eſſentials of true Holineſs; and the Spirit of Adoption, and Supplication, cauſeth us with Love to cry to God, and truſt him as a Father: They take Chriſt to be the only Mediator between God and Man, whoſe ſufficient Sacrifice for Sin, and perfect Righteouſneſs, Habitual, Active, and Paſſive (as called) advanced in dignity by the Divine Nature, is the Meritorious cauſe of all their Mercies to Body and Soul, Remiſſion, Juſtification, Holineſs, and Glory: They put up all their Services, as into, and by, the Hand of Chriſt; and from his Mediatory Hand they expect all mercies: They take the Holy Ghoſt within them to be Chriſt's

F   Ad-

Advocate and Witness to them of his Truth and Love; and their Witness, Earnest, Seal, Pledge, and first Fruits of endless Life: They take Eternal Glory for their full Felicity, and this World, and Flesh, (Pleasure, Riches, and Honour,) to be so far useful as they signifie Gods Love, and further our Love and Service to him; but to be *Vanity* as separated from God in our Hearts, and Enmity, or Mischief, as Competitors, or as against him. In a word, Faith working by Supream Love and Obedience to God, and Brotherly Love to Man, by Honour to our Superiours, Justice to all; and by all the good that we can do in the World, and by Repentance for our Sins, patience in sufferings, and by a Heavenly Mind, and Life, is the Sum of their Religion; or plainlier as is said at first, The Gospel-Covenant as expounded in the Creed, Lords-Prayer, and Decalogue, as the Summary of things to be believed, desired, and practised; and the holy Scriptures as the full and comprehensive Records of the Doctrine, Promises, and Laws of God, containing the Essentials, Integrals, and necessary Accidentals of Religion. This is the Christian Religion, and the Puritan in question is but the SERIOUS CHRISTIAN distinct from the HYPOCRITE, or dead Formalist.

But if you add *Non-conformity* to the sense of the Word, and to his Character; so I need not tell you what the Impositions are which some deny Conformity to, as to Oaths, New-Covenants, Subscriptions, Declarations, Practices, *&c.* which he protesteth that he would never deny Conformity to, if after his best enquiry he did not believe that God forbiddeth it: (As you may see at large in their *Savoy Petition for Peace* to the Bishops.) These two it seems you join together; and what their Objective Religion is, I have better told you, than you have
told

told your Relations. But as to the clearness of their Judgment in it, and the measure of their Practice of it, there are, I think, as various Degrees as there are Persons, no two Men in the World being in all things just of the same Degree.

And now Sir give me leave patiently to ask you these two Questions : 1. Why would you by temerity go about to deceive your Relations, and other Readers, by talking to them against that which you did not understand ? Even then, when you blame others as dealing so by the Papists ? And why do you dishonour your own Relations so, as to make so bad a Description of them? Are they such as have *no Love to God as God, no delight in Holiness, no Heavenly Minds*? *nothing almost but fear and its effects*? Have they *still the Flames of Concupiscence*, and greedy *desires of Money* and the *things of this Life, &c.* If it be not so, you should not have told the World so of them : If it be so, I am sorry for them : I suppose it is contrary to their profest Religion ; and you may have the greater hopes to make them Papists ?

II. What wonder is it that you that were no better a Puritan than you describe, are turned Papist ? You that profess you were a Puritan, must needs be judged to tell us what a one you were your self, when you tell us what they are? Alas poor Man ! How came you to be so false to your own Profession, against your Baptismal Vows, as to keep so much of the World at your Heart, in greedy desires after Money, and to have no more Love to God and Man ? no more Righteousness, Peace, and Joy in the Holy Ghost ? Could you think that a Man could be saved without *Love and good Works* ? Were you deluded by such *Antinomian* conceits as you describe, and took that for Puritanisme ? How else did you quiet your

Con-

Conscience in such a state of Hypocrisie? If God and Holiness had not your chief Love (as well as Fear) you were but an Hypocrite.

And here give me leave to repeat what I have oft written: What wonder is it at any Mans turning Papist? when according to your own Principles, no Protestant, Puritan, or other Christian turneth Papist, that doth not thereby declare that he was a false-hearted Hypocrite before, and had no true Love to God in his Heart: And was not this your case? For, 1. You affirm that all Men that have true prevalent Love to God are in a state of Grace, and have right to Salvation, (till they lose it:) 2. You affirm that none of us are in a state of Grace and Salvation, that are not of your Church, that is, the Subjects of the King, or Pope of *Rome*: 3. Therefore it followeth that you take none but such Subjects or Members of your Church, to have the true prevalent Love of God. But you know that in our Christian Covenant and Profession we all take God for our God, the infinite and most amiable Good, our Father in Christ, and Love it self, and that Faith working by Love is our Religion: *And if any Man*, saith Saint *Paul*, *love not the Lord Jesus Christ, let him be Anathema Maranatha*: And he *that loveth the World, the Love of the Father is not in him*, 1 *Joh*. 2. 15. So that by turning Papist you confess that before you were no true Christian, nor had any true Love to God and Godliness, nor to Jesus Christ: And if so, you were a false-hearted Hypocrite: For as a Christian you profest and Covenanted it. And what wonder then if God forsook you and gave you up to strong delusions, when you would not receive the Truth in the Love of it, that you might be saved, 2 *Thef*. 2.

And note here, that if any Man know that he truly
loveth

loveth God and Goodness, you tell him that he is none of those that you perswade to Popery: For you perswade none to it, but those that are ungodly Hypocrites, having no true Love of God within them.

But can you think, Sir, in good earnest, that Popery tendeth more to fill Men with the Love of God, than our simple Christianity doth? Is not Popery a Religion of Bondage and Servitude, consisting mainly in Terrour, and its superstitious effects? What are most of your Tasks of Pilgrimages, Penances, and abundance such, but the effects of servile fear? The best of Religion next Heaven should be that which is nearest to Heaven. And do you think you can love God better in the *Fire* of Purgatory Torments, than if he took you unto Christ in Paradise? Could you love God better in this Life, if he tormented you in the Fire, than if he give you comfort by his mercies?

You say that the Puritan [*is made negligent* (by his trust in Christ) *to adorn his Soul with Piety, Charity, Meekness, Patience, Humility, and other Christian Vertues; partly thinking them impossible to be attained, partly deeming there is no absolute necessity of them to his Salvation, he having nothing to do but to believe that Jesus Christ hath done all for him.*] *Answ.* I had hoped there had been few such left in *England*: Even *Crisp* and *Saltmarsh*, were scarce so erroneous: And *were you* such a one? O miserable Man that was such a Puritan! Who did bewitch you so grosly to contradict the whole Tenour of the Gospel? It is just with God to leave you, to set now as light by the *Meritorious Righteousness of Christ* as procuring you Pardon, Grace, and Glory, as you did then set by *Christian Virtues, Piety, and Love*? But what, if it was so with you, will that allow you to belie so many others? How many score Volumes have the Puritans written which assert not only the possibility, but the absolute necessity of Piety, Charity, Humility, &c. without which none can see God, (Infants Case is not here medled with.) I know not one Person in all the Land, or World, that will not abhor, as false, what you here charge in common on the Puritans, unless he be a very gross Antinomian, or some grosser Heretick here unknown: Protestants, Puritans, Separatists, Anabaptists, yea, Quakers, all abhor it: And yet you feared not to put this in Print? Perhaps you will pretend for it the Doctrine of Justification by Faith alone? But they that say that Faith alone going first with Repentance, doth justifie them, by procuring the pardon of their sins, and their Union with Christ, do say that at the same moment of time it also sanctifieth them, by procuring from Christ the Spirit of Sanctification, giving them Love, Humility, Piety, &c. And that this is of absolute necessity to their Salvation, Heb. 12. 14. Mat. 18. 3. Rom. 8. 1. 6. 7. 13. So much of your false self-condemning description of a Puritan.

CHAP. III.

II. YOU next Characterize the *Prelatical Protestant*: Having said before *p.5*. [*Their Preachers in their Sermons have little Life or Zeal; and seldom discourse of such Truths as are apt to awaken Mens Consciences, and make them lay to heart the great concern of the Salvation of their Souls. Or if they do at any time preach of Judgment, or of Hell, Repentance, or a New Life, they do it very*

very coldly and imperfectly, and seem to talk like Parrots, of what they have learnt by rote or out of others Books, and not what they have had any experience of in their hearts.] And *p. 6.* [*Generally speaking,* (*I wish it were a slander*) *Prelatick Protestants are very Prophane, and give no signs of any interiour trouble of Conscience: And if any of them begin to be heartily troubled for his sin, he is observed either to turn Fanatick or Papist.*]

Answ. If by a *Prelatick Protestant* you should unhandsomly mean only such as are *worldly Clergy-men*, like too many of your *Roman* Prelates and their Curates, who take Gain for Godliness, and who allow their Flesh, their Pride, their Covetousness, and Voluptuousness, and Sloth, to chuse their Religion; whose God is their Belly, who glory in their shame, and who mind Earthly things, and are Enemies to Cross-bearing; and through Enmity to those that are better than themselves, are Cross-imposers, and Persecutors, and Silencers, of sober faithful Ministers, because they cross their Pride and worldly Interest; such it's like may be no better Men than you describe them. But why should you take the Word in so narrow a sense?

But if by *Prelatick Protestants* you mean all such Protestants whose judgment is for Episcopacy, 1. You deceive, and I suppose are deceived, in your distinguishing these from *Non-conformists*: It's true that there are envious false-hearted Prelatists in the World, that make false names for their Brethren, to procure the belief of their false reports of them: And God will cut out the lying Tongue. But I will tell you the truth, whose malice soever is against it; there are *Episcopal* as well as *Presbyterian* and *Independent Non-conformists* now: Yea, divers that are against the late Wars of the Parliament, and against

against the Covenant, and never took it; and some that have been Souldiers for the King, and suffered for him: Yea so considerable is the number of them that are *Episcopal*, that in 1660. when the King called them to treat in order to agreement, they offered him *no other Form of Church Government, than A. Bishop* Usher's *Reduction*, in which not a *Pin of Honour*, nor one Farthing of *their Revenue* was desired to be taken from Archbishops, Bishops, Deans, Archdeacons; but only the Parish Ministers enabled under them, to have done somewhat more that belongeth to their Office, instead of Lay-Chancellors, *&c.* *Most Non-conformists* of my acquaintance would be glad of the terms contained in the Kings Declaration about Ecclesiastical Affairs, where Bishops and Archbishops are left as rich and high as they were before: So far are *Nonconformists* [*Episcopal Protestants.*]

2. And though *Conformity* be very much changed from what it was heretofore, *Episcopacy* is not. And I must tell you, that I do not think that the Christian World hath more godly learned worthy Ministers, than many of the Episcopal were heretofore. Do you know what men Bishop *Jewel*, A. Bishop *Grindall*, and many more of old were? And A. Bishop *Usher*, Bishop *Hall*, Bishop *Davenant*, and many more of late? Who hath written more earnestly and hotly for Episcopacy, than Bishop *Downame* (who wrote the great Latine Book to prove the Pope Antichrist;) yet who that knew him did ever question his piety or diligence? And if you look to the old Conformable Presbyters, read their Books, and enquire of the Lives of many of them, and then confess that they were better men and better Preachers than you describe. Peruse the Writings of Mr. *Rob. Bolton, William Whateley, William Fenner,* Dr. *Preston,* Dr. *Sibbes,* Dr. *Stoughton,*
Dr.

Dr. *Gouge*, Mr. *Thomas Gataker*, Mr. *Crook*, and abundance of such others, and enquire how they laboured and lived, and you may hear that they were neither such *Parrots* nor *prophane* ones as you mention.

There may be some proportionable alteration supposed to be now made in the persons of the Conformists, answerable to that which is made in Conformity it self: But surely, if you know *London*, and many Miles near it, and many Parishes in the several Counties, you must confess that now there are many Learned, Pious Conformists, who Preach zealously, and live religiously, and hate Covetousness and Persecution, and long to see the promoting of Piety, Peace, and Concord.

But if you expect a better Vindication of them, I must desire you to consider of two things. 1. That in most Countries and Ages the *worldliest men* (that is, the *worst*) have been the greediest strivers and seekers for Church-Power and Preferments; and he that seeketh most diligently is the likeliest to find: And that ordinarily the Vulgar do dance after the Pipe of him that is uppermost, and will be of the Religion of them that can help or hurt them, be it what it will be. Most will be of the Religion which is owned by Law, or countenanced by the Greatest, be it right or wrong. In the best Countries, the most are too bad: And bad men will have a prospering Religion, and not one that will expose them to Death, Banishment, Imprisonment, Beggary, Contempt, or Silence. Most will be on the upper side.

2. And remember that you your self here confess the scandals of some of your Romish Party, and what carnal prophane ones they are. Had you not confessed it, I would have desired you to read two Books. 1. *Josep. Acosta*, of the wicked slothful Priests in the *Indies*, as

G the

the great hindrance of their Converſion. 2. *Stephanus* his World of Wonders, taken moſt out of the Book of the Queen of *Navarre*, of the horrid Villanies of your Prieſts.

And one thing I cannot diſregard: I marvel not if the Papiſts be moſt bad in *Spain*, *France*, *Italy*, &c. or the *Lutherans* in *Denmark*, *Saxony*, or *Sweden*; or the *Calviniſts* in *Holland*; or the Prelatiſts and Conformiſts in *England*; becauſe the *moſt* (who are commonly the *worſt*) will be of the ſtronger ſide. But that *Greeks* ſhould be ungodly in *Turky*, or *Proteſtants* in *France*, or *Papiſts* in *England*, where they are *ſingular*, and under the diſcountenance of the Times, and moſt hold their Religion with ſome *ſelf-denyal*, this ſeemeth to me a more grievous thing. And if it prove true, that even in *England*, where you make the World believe that you have ſuffered grievouſly, your Followers are too often found meer *Formaliſts*, living in Swearing, Drinking, Lying, Uncleanneſs, or ſome of *theſe*, what ſhall we think of ſuch a Religion as this, as in a Land of uprightneſs would teach men to do unjuſtly? I wonder not what ſhould make a Drunkard, Fornicator, or other debaucht Sinner to be a Papiſt in *France*, *Spain*, or *Italy*: But what ſhould make ſuch a one be a Papiſt in *England*, unleſs his Religion favour ſenſuality, *or elſe* he think that it will yet prove the upper ſide, I cannot eaſily conjecture.

But you accuſe the *Prelatick Proteſtant* for *agreeing with the Puritan in expecting Salvation by the extrinſical righteouſneſs of Chriſt without him, not by any interior righteouſneſs in his own Soul.*] *Anſw.* I told you your memory faileth you: Why did you before then deſcribe the Puritan as ſo well qualified within, and deſiring after more? But were you bred among Puritans, and yet talk ſo ignoranly and falſly? This had been more tolerable in

a *Cochleus*, a *Genebrard*, or other tranſmarine Calumniator, that never knew us here. Read but *Davenant de Juſt.* and ſee how you ſlander the Conformiſts. And read my fore-named Books, and Mr. *Trumans*, Mr. *Woodbridges*, the Morning Lectures at S. *Giles* of *Juſtif.* Mr. *Wotton de Reconciliat.* Mr. *Bradſhaw de Juſtif. Præfat. &c.* Mr. *Gataker* in many Books, *Jo. Goodwin* of Juſtif. &c. and ſee how you ſlander the Puritans. In a few plain words, Sir, the Proteſtants do not expect Salvation by their own perſonal righteouſneſs as coordinate with Chriſts, but as ſubordinate to it, nor as a Righteouſneſs ſo denominated from the ſame *Reaſon* as Chriſts is, but from a lower Reaſon, and ſo as of a lower ſort. That is,[" We all hold, that " Gods Law to perfect man was perfect, being the Effect " of his perfect Holineſs, and required perſonal perpetual " perfect innocency and obedience in man: And that " man breaking this Law, was according to the Juſtice of " it lyable to its Penalty, which is temporal, ſpiritual, and " eternal death, or to be forſaken of that God whom he " forſook, and to be under the ſenſe of his diſpleaſure, or " Juſtice: We believe that Chriſt Redeemed us from this " Puniſhment, by the merit of his perfect Holineſs and " Obedience, and the ſatisfactory ſacrificing of himſelf " on the Croſs, where he was in his meaſure forſaken " of God, as in our ſtead and for our ſins; whoſe pu" niſhment, as far as was fit for him to undergo, he vo" luntarily undertook to ſuffer. We believe that he ne" ver intended by this Redemption, to take man from " under his ſubjection to God, or make him an ungovern" ed lawleſs Wight; but that by purchaſe he himſelf, as " Mediator, became his Lord and King, and Gods chief " Adminiſtrator of the Redeemed World: And his Lord" Redeemer, with the Will and Authority of God his
" Creator,

"Creator, made him a new Law and Covenant, *freely* "*giving Right to Impunity* (saving paternal healing Cor- "rections, and temporal death, and degrees of desertion "if men neglect Grace) and *Right* to the *Heavenly Glory,* "as thus merited for us by Christ; and also the Com- "munion of the Holy Ghost on Earth, to fit us by Holi- "ness for Heaven, and to conquer our sins; and this to "all that will by a true effectual Faith, accompanyed with "Repentance, unfeignedly accept the Gift of God, that "is, that will truly consent to the Baptismal Covenant, "taking God for their reconciled God and Father, Jesus "Christ for their Saviour, and the Holy Ghost for their "Sanctifier and Comforter, renouncing the Devil, the "World, and the Flesh, and engaging themselves as in "a Holy War against them, as the Enemies of the bles- "sed Trinity, and them. And this Covenant they must "keep: For as it giveth Right to Life to such Believers, so "it denounceth certain damnation to Unbelievers and un- "thankful Neglecters of so great Salvation.

"So that when by [RIGHTEOUSNESSE] we "mean that which answereth Gods perfect Law, having "no sinful imperfection, we all profess that we have no "such Righteousness of our own to trust in, there being "no man without sin; and all sin by the Law of Inno- "cency denominating the sinner unrighteous and punish- "able by death: But instead of such a Righteousness, "Gods Justice is so far satisfied by the Sacrifice and per- "fect Righteousness of Christ, as that he freely giveth "us the foresaid Covenant, and its Free Grace and Bene- "fits: But because we must be judged by the Redeemer "according to his Law of Grace, therefore we must in "our selves personally have the Righteousness which that "Law or Covenant hath made necessary to our Justification

"cation first, and our Salvation afterwards; which is first
"our foresaid Faith or Covenant-Consent, and after (to
"our salvation) our keeping of that Covenant in true
"Obedience and Holiness to the end, and our Victory
"over the three Enemies which we renounced. So that
"briefly, God justifieth as the Donor and the Judge;
"Christ God and Man, as Mediator, justifieth us *merito-*
"*riously*, as aforesaid, and by *donation* and *final* sentence;
"our *Jus ad Impunitatem & Gloriam*, our Right to *Impu-*
"*nity* and the *Heavenly Glory*, justifieth us as our *Formal*
"*Righteousness* (which is a Relation) against the Accusa-
"tion that we ought to be shut out of Heaven and damn-
"ed to Hell. The Covenant of Grace justifieth us, by
"giving us Right to the Love of the Father, the Grace
"of the Son, and the Communion of the Holy Ghost:
"Even as Gods Donative and Condonative Instrument,
"or Act of Grace. Our Personal Faith including Repen-
"tance justifieth us, as the matter of our Formal Righte-
"ousness, against that particular Accusation, that we
"are *Impenitent Unbelievers*, and so have no part in
"Christ and his Covenant Gift. And our sincere, though
"imperfect, Holiness added to our Faith, is our material
"Righteousness, against that particular Accusation, that
"we are unholy, and so unqualified for Heaven: So that
"the formal Nature of Righteousness being Relative,
"and the word having various senses according to the
"variety of respects, and all these fore-mentioned ha-
"ving their several parts or offices, to the Being of our
"final perfect Justification, all these may accordingly be
"the Reasons of our expectation of salvation. I forgot
"to adde, that we are so far justified by the *Holy Ghost* also,
"as he is the Author of this Holiness, which is our ne-
"cessary qualification for eternal life. 1 *Cor.* 6. 19, 11.
Tit. 3. 3, 4, 5.   I have

I have here truly, diftinctly, and plainly told you the Proteftant and Puritan, that is, the *Chriftian Doctrine* of Juftification.

As to the fenfe of the word [*Imputing*] fee how we do, or do not own it, briefly in Mr. *Bradſhaw's* Preface, or largely in my *Treat. of Juftifying Righteoufneſs and Imputation*. And in my *Cathol. Theolog*. I have done you and Chriftianity the fervice, to prove by plain Citations, that many of your Learnedeft Divines do fay herein the fame as we, or very little differ from us; and if you will as a Make-bate prove the contrary, you will do it to the Diffenters fhame. If you truft not Chrift alone, as we do, you will find the want of a Saviour in your neceffity, and Purgatory will not ferve your turn.

But you tell us, that [*Some of the Prelatick Clergie begin to fcoff at the Doctrine of Imputative Juſtice: One of them lately, in a Sermon before his Majefty, called it, and not improperly, the Mummery of Imputative Juſtice*.] I will tranfcribe no more of your Scoff: It's dangerous mocking at fuch matters: *Imputed Righteoufneſs* is oft mentioned by the Holy Ghoft in Scripture. It is not fome mens mif-expofition that will juftifie your derifion. It's no ftrange thing for men of undigefted thoughts on both fides, publickly and privately to revile at each other as erroneous, when if they had but the skill of fpeaking diftinctly, and underftanding one another, they would prefently profefs that they are agreed; or if it be for want of underftanding the matter, it's pity but they fhould be quiet till they underftand it. I am of their mind that think it is here fafeft to keep clofe to Scripture phrafe; for want of which many wrangle about their own ambiguous or ill-made words, that in the matter difagree not.

But,

But, Sir, when you say, pag.6. [*An Imputative holy man is a meer Christmas Mummer ;*] And after your jeasting "*with the Boys and Girls, and the Coblers and Botchers Regal Attire, and the Daw and her fine Feathers, you conclude [such will be the sad Lot of meerly Imputative Saints, who to themselves and their Brethren seem very fine in the extrinsical Righteousness of Christ, put on by their phantastical Faith, whilst God and his Angels under all this conceited assumed Bravery see a lascivious, wanton, covetous Miser.*] I must crave leave to call upon your Conscience, to judge whether a man that professeth that while he seemed a Puritan he was *but an unholy, lascivious, wanton, and covetous miser*, and since his turning Papist tells the World in Print, that he is now a *most false calumniator*, be a fit person to invite his Relations to such a pitiful change, to save their Souls? While you talkt but of [*Imputative Justice*] some mens ambiguous words gave you an excuse: For some Protestants think that nothing should be called *Justifying Righteousness*, which is not sinless and perfect: But this is but a Controversie about a *word* or *Name* of Righteousness. But when you here pretend, that they are for *meerly Imputed Holiness*, I must say that I remember not that ever I read a more impudent Slander: And he that will dwell in Gods holy Hill must not receive a false Report, especially in despight of the fullest evidence that man can desire: Are not our Booksellers Shops full of Books for the necessity of personal Holiness? and that none can be saved but Saints? Is it not one of our dislikes of your Way, that Saints must be made rare Canonized Persons, when all Christians hold, that without Holiness none shall see God? When almost all the Sermons that ever I heard Preached by any man of sense in my life profess this, and almost

all

all our Books are on this very subject, who would have thought that a man on earth could have been found, that would deny it in the open face of the Sun? Yea, one that saith he was a Puritan, and an University Student? Even when the poor Puritans are ruined, and hunted about, and cast into Goals, becaufe they dare not give over preaching the *necessity of Personal Holiness to salvation* (for that is the most of all their Sermons that ever I heard) dare you stand forth with such an accusation as this? as if they held no Holiness necessary but Imputative? Why then are we devoted in Baptism to the Holy Ghost? Yea what are the very Separatists more accused of, than that they would have none but real Saints in their Communion, too far presuming to judge the Heart? You seem a zealous man, though very ignorant; I pray you study not to excuse this, but let us hear that you as openly repent as you have sinned.

The most of your further dealing with the *Prelatick Protestant*, is to tell him that his Ritual Principles lead him to turn Papist, or else he cannot answer the Puritan: I take not my self any further fit to interpofe herein, than to tell you, that in all things truly Indifferent, there is a just middle between any mistaken Scruplers that hold them sinful, and a Papist that maketh them a part of his Christianity or Religion, and will not be of the same Religion and Church with those that be not of his mind, nor will willingly suffer them to preach or live. I told you that S. *Paul* and the Churches described by *Socrates* and *Sozomen* (about *Easter*) were of this middle way: They neither thought Liturgies or Ceremonies so bad (or unlawful at all,) as some on one side called Puritans do, nor so necessary as to make them a Partition-Wall between Churches and Churches, or to forbid Communion,

or

or the Preaching of Chrifts Gofpel, or Chriftian Peace, to thofe that differ about them. And I think this middle way is approved by God and Angels, and by many at death, or after long experience, who were againft it before in profperity and paffion.

The Inftances which you give, are, I. That [*the Prelatick Proteftant is very angry with the Puritan, that he will not abftain from Flefh in* Lent, *on* Frydays, Emberdays, *and* Vigils *of Saints----Though practically fpeaking no body takes lefs notice of them than himfelf----And the poor Puritan, becaufe he will not folemnly invite the People to obferve, what himfelf never intends to take the leaft notice of, muft for this be filenced and fufpended both from Office and Benefice.*]

Anfw. 1. Here you fhew what things they be that you turn Papift for: Is not eating Flefh on *Frydays, Lent*, or *Vigils,* a worthy matter to make another Religion of, or to prove men to be of differing Churches?

2. I told you before, that the Puritans judgment is as *Paul*'s, that fuch things fhould be left indifferent, or at leaft make no breach among us; by our *judging* or *defpiſing* one another: And that neither the Pope, nor any men on Earth, have Authority to make Univerfal Laws for them to all the Chriftian World; and that there is no true Tradition of Apoftolical Inftitution of them: But yet that fuch Fafts and Feafts as are appointed by true Authority of Prince or Paftors, not againft the Laws of God, and fuch as fhall be proved to be inftituted by the Apoftles, they will obferve.

3. But the *poor Puritan* is indeed in hard Circumftances, were there no life after this! Some of them have no Flefh to eat, either on *Frydays*, or any day in the Week, but live thankfully upon Bread and Milk, and fome fuch things;

things; Fish they would gladly eat, if they could get it. There are now among them such as with many. Children have for a long time lived almost only on brown Rye-bread and Water: Many of them take it for a sufficient quantity to eat one temperate Meal a day, though they are in no want; and the Papist that forbeareth Flesh, and eateth better than the Puritan feasteth with, or that fasteth with one Meal a day, which is many Puritans fullest Dyet, doth condemn the poor Puritan as an Heretick, and perhaps burn him at a Stake, or cast him into the Inquisition, for not Fasting. Poor *John Calvin* did eat but one small Meal a day, and the Papist who fast much at the rate as *Calvin* feasted, record him for a gluttonous person. And so did the Pharisees by Christ and his Disciples; *why do not thy Disciples fast, &c.*

II. Your second Instance is, [*The Prelatick Protestant wonders the Puritan should scruple adorning the Communion Table, with two Wax Tapers, &c.*]

Ans. The former Answer serveth to this: Hear, O ye Puritans, wherein the *Roman* Religion doth surpass yours! Their Altars have lighted *Tapers* on: Do you not deserve to be burnt your selves, if you will not burn Candles on your Altars?

Yea the Pope, who hath power to set up and take down Emperours and Kings, being not only the King of *Rome*, but the Monarch of the whole World, doth appoint these Lights as a Professing *sign* [" *before God and Man*, " *that he is of that Church which in the Primitive Times* " *for fear of Persecution served God by Candle-light in* " *Dens and Caves*,] And is not this to prove the *immutability* of their Church, that vary not in a *Circumstance* from the *Apostolical Institution*? Doth his domineering over Kings and Nations, and the Hosts of Great Princes,

Cardinals,

Cardinals, Prelates, Abbots, Clergy, Regulars, Seculars, that obey him, shew also that he is of that *old Candle-lighted Church*?

But while you seem still to plead *Apostolical Tradition* for all these Great Parts of your Religion, tell the poor Puritan, whether it was by Prophesie, or how else, that the Apostles delivered to the Church the use of these *Lighted Tapers*, in commemoration of that which was done in *Dens* long after the death of these Apostles? I doubt rather, the Pope doth by this practice condemn himself, and sets up these Lights to shew the World how much he and his Church are changed since those forementioned days.

III. You next say, [*The Prelatick Protestant wonders what hurt the Puritan can see in making the sign of that on the forehead of a new baptized Infant, yet smiles at a Papist when he makes it on himself, or his Victuals, &c.*]

Ans. None of us are ashamed of the Cross of Christ, nor loth to profess this as openly as you: But if we do it by *word*, by *writing*, by *Obeying*, or by *Suffering*, we are of another Religion from you, (it seems by you,) unless we will do it also by *crossing*: The *Jews* were the *Cross-makers*: And there are now so many *Cross-makers* in the World, whose Trade we like not, that we are not forward to set up *their sign* at *our doors*. But yet there are Puritans and Prelatists, that were they among the Deriders of a Crucified Christ, where the use were not a Formality, or worse, but convenient to tell the Infidels their mind, that they are *not ashamed of the Cross of Christ*, would not refuse seasonably to Cross themselves. But the Puritans think, that when it is made [*a solemn stated sign of the Duty and Grace of the New Covenant, dedicating thereby the person to God, as one hereby obliging him-*

self

self to profess the Faith of Christ Crucified, and manfully to fight under his Banner against the Devil, the World, and the Flesh to the death, *in hope of the Benefits of his Cross and Covenant, and so is made a Badge or Symbol of our Christianity,*] then it is made a *Sacrament of the Covenant of Grace*, *added to Christs Sacrament of the same use*; or at least *too like it*, though the *Name* be denyed it: And they think that Christ hath given none power to make *such new Sacraments or Symbols of Christianity*; he having done that sufficiently himself. They have a conceit that the King would not be pleased with them that either frame a new *Oath of Allegiance* added to his, as the *Badge* of his *Subjects Loyalty*, nor yet that would make a new *Badge* of the *Order of the Knights of the Garter*, without his consent. At least, the Puritans think that *Baptism, and Christianity, and Christian Burial should not be denyed to those Children, whose Parents do not offer them to be baptized with this additional Symbol*: And if the poor men be deceived in such thoughts, it is but in fear of sinning against Christ, and not that they are more ashamed of his Cross than you, or more disobedient to Authority.

IV. Your next instance is, [*The Prelatick Protestant wonders that the Puritane can doubt the holy Eucharist is really and truly the body of Christ*, &c.] And you cite Dr. *Cosins Hist. Transub. p.* 44.

Answ. 1. The *Prelatick Protestant* and the *Puritane* differ not at all about the real presence of Christs body in the Sacrament, as I have shewed you elsewhere. What need you more proof than King *Edwards* old Rubrick against the Real Presence in a gross sence, lately restored to the Liturgie. And as for Dr. *Cosins* words and book, I again tell you, all the Doctors of the Roman Church are

are never able to answer his full proof that Transubstantiation is a late innovation; and none of the doctrine of the ancient Churches. We challenge you all to give any reasonable answer to that book: And you still Cunningly bawke the main Controversie between us and you, which is not whether *Christs Body be* there, but whether *Bread and Wine be* there. For I have told you, 1. That we who know not how far a Glorified Spiritual Body is extensive and invisible to us, cannot tell you where it is present or absent, no more than of an Angel. 2. But we all hold, as a piece of Plate or Silver Barrs, is really and truly turned into the Kings Coine, so the Bread and Wine is really and truly turned into Christs *Sacramental Body and Blood*; and yet one is *Silver* and the other is *Bread and Wine* still: The change is *true, but Relative* by its Separation to that holy use: as a Common person may be Really Changed into a *King*, or a *Lord*, or a *Judge*, or a *Captain*, or a *Bishop*, or a *Doctor*, and yet be a *man* still. This *real* change we all Confess. But the question is, whether there be *no Bread*.

V. You say [*The Prelatick Protestant wonders that the Puritan when he is going out of this world should find difficulty to make a particular Confession of his sins, if any grievous matter lye on his Conscience, and humbly desire the Prelatick Priests absolution, saying &c*].

Answ. I know of no difference between the Prelatist and the Puritan about *Confession* or *Absolution*. Dr. John *Reynolds* a true Puritan, received *Absolution* before he dyed: Meer Puritans believe that it is a duty to Confess our sins to men. 1. In Case of such injury to any as must have a Confession towards the injured persons *Satisfaction* and *forgiveness*. 2. In Case of such difficulty about either the nature of the *sin*, or *Consequent dangers* or *dutyes*, as

make

make a particular Guide neceſſary, who cannot reſolve our doubts till he know the Caſe. 3. In Caſe that the Conſcience be ſo burdened with the ſin, as that the ſinner cannot by other means find eaſe, till he have disburdened himſelf by ſuch Confeſſion. 4. In Caſe it be neceſſary to heal any ſcandal given to others; It is a very great duty for drunkards, fornicators, deceivers, and ſuch others to go to their Companions, and lament their ſin, and perſwade them no more to do as they have done: And if required by the Paſtors to take publick ſhame before the Congregation, and acknowledg that the doctrine of Chriſt never countenanced them in any ſuch ſin, that Religion and the Church may not bear the reproach of their delinquency. And to beg the prayers of the Congregation for their pardon, and that the Paſtor by virtue of his office will pronounce it.

But we are not aſhamed to confeſs that neither Puritans nor Prelatiſts think it lawful to make the people believe that they muſt needs tell the Prieſt of all the ſins that they commit, and dutyes that they omit; Nor to uphold pragmatical Prieſts in the trade of knowing all mens thoughts and ſecret actions, even Princes, by which they may betray them. 1. The number of people and of their ſins, is ſo great as render it impoſſible: In this Pariſh it's thought there is above threeſcore thouſand ſouls: How many thouſand ſinful thoughts, or words or deeds a great part of theſe may commit in a year, I leave to your Conjecture: only I muſt tell you that if all men High and Low, that are called Papiſts about us, ſhould but tell the Prieſt of every time they are drunk, and every Fornication they have committed, every prophane Oath they have ſworn, every Lye they have told, (eſpecially againſt the Proteſtants,) and of every filthy and prophane Word
that

that they have spoken, and every Oppression of the poor, and every filthy or covetous thought that hath been in their hearts, they had need of a very Traditional Memory to remember them, or great plenty of Ink and Paper to record them, and a whole Diocess of Clergy-men in one Parish to hear them. How many hundred Priests must this Parish have, if all should thus confess all sins of Commission and Omission? every cold Prayer, and omitted Prayer, Exhortation, Alms, Example, &c. especially the great Omissions of the Soul, in the defects of the exercise of Faith, Hope, Love, and Patience, &c.

2. And what good will it do a man, that is himself of sound understanding and integrity, to open his Conscience to an ignorant or unconscionable man, that will call evil good, and good evil, and will put him upon sin; as you here do by your Relations; or that dare himself sin as boldly as you here do, when you accuse Puritans and Prelates as holding *meer Imputed Holiness*.

3. And how great a temptation and injury may this be to your Priests, in such instances as *Montaltus* the *Jansenist* mentioneth, with which I will not defile my Paper? when, alas! most of them are not men fit to bear such temptations: What if twenty thousand People in one Parish should each make this Confession to a Papist Priest, [*I am afraid I have sinned in believing the common Report, that you are a very ignorant drunken sot, and a common whoremaster, and a proud, covetous, lying man;*] would it not be like to enrage the Priest into an enmity against his Flock? If all the Fornicators in such a Parish should tell such Priests of all their filthy thoughts, and words, and their *immodest actions*, and *actual Fornications*, how like were it to make such impressions on the poor Priests Phantasie, as would pollute him with many filthy imaginations.   VI. You

VI. You adde, [*The Prelatick Protestant wonders at the Puritan's niceness, that he can by no means be perswaded to bow at the Name of Jesus: When Nature teacheth us a Relative Reverence, &c. The sound of the Name Jesus is vanished and gone, before the superstitious Worshipper can make his mimical Congie: whereas the Picture, a far more lively representation of the same great Lord, remains.*]

Ans. 1. The Puritans think it not unlawful to bow when God or Jesus are named. But, 1. They are loth to serve those men, that would turn all serious Religion into a dead Image of it. 2. And they like not bowing at the Name Jesus, and not at the Name [*God*], or [*Christ*], or *Immanuel*, or *Jehovah*, or the *Holy Ghost*.]

2. As to Images, I will but refer you to Dr. *Stillingfleet*'s last Book against *Godwin*, which hath fully proved, that you use them as truly Idolatrously as did the Heathens.

VII. Your next Instance is, [The *Conformists* rejecting the Popish *Girdle*, *Stole*, and *Casuble*, and yet wondring at the *Puritans* rejecting the *Surplice*.]

Ans. The former Answers serve to this: Some *Puritans* would use the Surplice, if that would serve and satisfie. But they see, that if they say [*A*] first, they must say [*B*] next, and so on to the end of your Alphabet. But still you tell us what great things your new Religion doth consist of, and what great cause you had to turn from the Puritans to the Papists? If you had known no more than Books can tell you, and your Grandfather had not known better than *Baronius* himself, what the Apostles did and instituted, we should never have known that the Religion which is integrated by a *Surplice*, *Girdle*, *Stole*, and *Casuble*, had been herein Apostolical, and not rather a novel thing.

VIII. Your

VIII. Your eighth Instance is about *praying for the dead*: But whatever you say of the Rector of S. *Martins* in *Oxford*, there is no difference between the *Puritans* and the *Prelatick Protestants* in that point: You mistake the matter: It is *another passage*, or *two* or *three* at Burial, which the Puritan sticks at, *viz.* which pronounceth of every individual person in the Kingdom, Atheists, Infidels, Papists, and Impenitent Sinners that we bury, except only the *Excommunicate*, *Unbaptized*, and *Self-murderers*, that [*God of his mercy hath taken to himself the Soul of this our dear Brother, out of the miseries of this sinful life, &c.*]

IX. Your last Instance indeed toucheth the quick of our Controversie with *Rome:* You say[*The Prelatick Protestant wonders at the Puritan's Pride, that he will not submit his judgment in matters of Faith, to the determination of a Council of all the Reverend Bishops of the Land, his Majesty as Supreme Head and Governour presiding,*] yet submit not [*to the determination of a General Council of all the Learned Bishops of the Christian World, his Holiness the Pope as Supreme Pastor presiding, and believe as the Universal Church of Christ believeth: It's fitting, says the Conformist, that for Order sake in Christs Church, there should be in every Nation some Supreme Governours, to whose Directions in matters of Divine worship, all should submit; else we shall have as many Christian Religions and ways of Worship, as there are Parishes, Families, or Persons. The Puritan replyeth, It seems as rational that Christ should for the same Reasons of conserving union, decency, and order in his Church, appoint one Supreme Pastor over all Christians, dispersed in all the Nations of the world, whom all should obey in the vacancy of General Councils.*]

Ans. This deserveth our wakeful Remarks: I. So your
sacred

sacred Cardinal *Bertrand* (in *Biblioth. Patrum*) said, that *God had not been wise else, if he had not placed one Supreme, as his Vicar over the world*. And so you can tell what *God hath done*, by your superlative Wit which can tell us what he *ought to do*. God doth all wisely: But if he had not made an Universal Head of the World under him, he had not done wisely; *ergo*, he hath made such an Head, *&c*. This is Historical Logick.

II. But is this Monarch the Head in *Civil* Government, or only in *Ecclesiastick*? Why is your *One Church* no more *One* in answering this Question? Nay why were poor *Barclay, Withrington*, and such others, whose Writings *Goldastus* hath preserved, so hardly judged of, for pleading for Kings Supremacy in Civil Government? And if you are of their mind, tell us if you can, why God must not be judged as unreasonable and unwise, if he have not made *One Universal Civil Monarch of all the World*? I undertake, when you will come to a due tryal, to prove, that *Civil Government* is such as may as well, and *far better*, be done by *Officers* and *Deputies* than the *Ecclesiastical Government* can: And I pray who is the Uuniversal Monarch? Or who must be he? Or how must he be chosen? I would have our King have no mortal King set over him, at least without a chusing Vote. And shall they meet in a General Council of Kings to chuse one? By that time the Place and Time be agreed on, and the Kings have all left their Kingdoms, and be come from the *Antipodes*, and the *Terra Australis incognita*, and all other Kingdoms to that Council to chuse a Monarch of the World, they will be too old to return home again. Or shall they fight it out, till one have Conquered all the rest? Alas, who shall bear the charge of the Conquest at the *Antipodes*, and who shall answer for all the Blood?

When

When one cannot get all *Europe* at a cheaper rate, than will be expressed by many Kingdoms groans, and the Soil dunged with mens flesh and blood. I have long ago on this subject given (in my *Key for Catholicks*) an Answer to *Richlieu*, and to *Carol. Boverius*, who wrote for the Honour of Ecclesiastick Monarchy, from the similitude of Civil, to have perverted our late King; as if he would have made him believe, that the World must have one mortal Monarch.

Contrarily, If it be *Madness and Hostility to all Kings and States, for any one man on earth to claim and seek to be the Monarch of all the World in Civil Government, it is madness and hostility to Kings, Pastors, and People, for any one man to claim and seek to be the Monarch of all the world in Ecclesiastick Government. But the former is true: Ergo, so is the latter.* I am ready to make good the Comparison.

III. But, Sir, if the Pope be S. *Peter's* Successor, is not his *Apostolick office* as Universal as his *Monarchy* or Ruling office? Surely the *first part* of the *Apostles office* was to preach and *baptize*, and *make Christians* and *gather Churches*, and the Governing of them was but the second part: And is the Pope the *Apostle* of all the world? Then it seemeth that he is a betrayer of most of the whole earth to the Devil, that neither preacheth to them *per se vel per alios*. But S. *Peter's* Charge was not *Vniversal* but *Indefinite*. And even as to *Government*, why did he never so much as send his Deputies to govern the Abassins for so many hundred years? Nay hence it seemeth to follow, that all the preaching and Church-order that hath been for so many hundred years, either there or in any other Nation, by which millions have been turned to Christianity and edified, without the mission or

Commission of the Roman Monarch, should have been left undone; and all was unlawful?

IV. But must your *Pope* be obeyed as Supreme but in the *Vacancy of General Councils*? Dare you preach this at *Rome*? 1. How then come the Councils of *Constance* and *Basil* for such Doctrine to be *unapproved or reprobate Councils*? How came Pope *Eugenius* to keep up and continue the succession, when so great a General Council had deposed him as Heretical, Simoniacal, and many ways flagitious? 2. And what? Have we a Catholick Church with two Heads? that are *per vices* the Vicars of Christ? A *Pope* one year, and a *Council* another? Then sure they are *two Churches*, seeing the *Pars imperans* is the *specifying part*. 3. But the best is, it is at the Pope's will, whether ever there shall be a General Council more? And he knoweth which side his Bread is Buttered on? Nay, they say, no Decree is valid without his approbation: And if ever a *John*, or *Eugenius* of them all will approve of his own Deposition for Heresie, Simony, Adultery, &c. he is not the Man that I took him for. 4. But if the name [*General Council*] be not a Cheat, and taken for a Council very far from being General, as to the *whole Christian world*, let the Pope set his heart at rest; I will undertake to secure him from the danger of such a Council, and to prove that such there never *ought* to be, *will be*, or *can be*, unless Christianity come much nearer to be rooted out of the Earth, and the Church brought into a narrower room.

V. But you have a reflecting Comparison between the *Kings presiding* and the *Popes*, and between a *National Council* and the *Bishops of the whole Christian World*. To begin at the later part: Alas poor *ignorant Man*, if you believe this your self? And alas *unfaithful Man*, if if you believe it not and yet dare say it? Do you yet know no difference between the *orbis Romanus*, and the *orbis universalis*? Or will you with *William Johnson*, alias *Terret*, prove your Councils to be Universal, because such places as *Thracia* had Bishops there, as if *Thracia* had been without the Empire? or because such a name as *Johannes Persidis* is found at *Nice*? Read all the subscribed names, and return to a sounder mind! *Theodoret* knew what he said, when he gave the reason why *James* Bishop of *Nisibis* in *Persia*, or near it, was at the Council of *Nice*, *Because* Nisibis *was then under the* Roman *Emperour*.

Do you not know that most of the Christian World (two to one) are not of the Pope's Subjects; and are *All the Bishops of the Christian World* then on your side? And do you not know that when *Constantine* presided at *Nice*, his Dominion was full as large as the Bishop of *Rome*'s was, and a little larger.

VI. But because you shall find us reasonable, we will tell you, that we consent to General Councils where the Pope consenteth not? We consent to what the great Councils at *Calcedon* and *Constantinople*, before mentioned, say of the *Humane Institution of his Primacy*, and the *Reason* and *Mutability* of it; and so doth not the Pope? We consent to the Councils at *Constance*, *Basil*, *Pisa*, that the Pope may be deposed as a Heretick, and worse; but the Pope doth not: Is it not he then that dissenteth from *all the Bishops of the world*?

VII. And for the Kings presiding we wholly own it: He is the Governour of *Clergy-men*, as well as of Physicians; and he is to see that they abuse not their Function

to

to the common hurt. The difference is here, 1. Our King Governeth but his own Dominions: But your Pope would Govern all the World. 2. Our King hath an undoubted Title: Your Pope is an Usurper. 3. And as to your name [*Head*] he hath given the World full satisfaction, that he did never claim to be a *Priest-Head* or *Governour*, a *Constitutive* Head of a *properly called Church*, nor to have the power of *word, Sacraments*, and *Keys*, so as to administer them; but to be a Civil *Head* and Governour of Priests, and the Churches in his Dominions; as he is of Physicians, *&c.*

VIII. And you mistake the Puritans, if you think they are not for this Government: Why else take they the Oath of Supremacy? Yea, and if you think that they are not for as much Unity and Concord of all the Churches in a Kingdom, as can be had without a greater hurt, than the lesser particularities of their concord will do good: And they are not against National Synods for such Concord: And they hold the King to be the *Regular Head or Governour*, or Principium *of that Concord*: But not *principium essentiale ipsius Ecclesiæ*: And therefore the Puritans differ from judicious *Ric. Hooker*, who faith, [*If the King be the Head of the Church, he must needs be a Christian*:] For we hold that an *Infidel King* may be so the Head, that is, the *Rightful Governour* of the Christians and Churches in his Dominion; or else how should they be obliged to obey him?

IX. And you are mistaken, if you think that the Puritans and the Prelatists differ about submitting our Faith to the judgment of the Church: We subscribe the same Articles, which say that General Councils may erre, and have erred, even about matters of Faith.

X. But I must tell you, that the Puritans, who are accused

cused of *disorder* and *confusion*, do many of them loath *disorder* and *confusion*, even in *words* and *doctrine*. And they distinguish here between the *Churches keeping* and *teaching* the Christian Faith, and the *Churches judging in matters of Faith*. The first they are wholly for: We must receive our Faith from our Teachers, and *oportet discentem fide humana credere*. But if by *Judging* you mean strictly a *Decisive judgment*, in which we must rest, which way soever the sentence pass, as if the Church might not only teach us the truth of our Religion, but judge *in partem utramlibet*, whether it be true or not, the Puritans own no such power in the Church, nor will so submit their Faith to the judgment of it. They believe that Pastors in Councils have power to judge that there is a God, Almighty, *&c.* a Christ, a Holy Ghost, that Christ dyed, rose, *&c.* that the Scripture is true, that there is an absolute necessity of Holiness, that there is a Resurrection and Life everlasting, that Gods Commandments must be kept, and sin not committed, *&c.* But that no Council hath power to judge that there is no God, no Christ, or the contrary to any one of these, or any other revealed Truth of God.

XI. And I must not let pass your Schismatical inference, that [*else there should be as many Religions and ways of worship as Parishes or persons*] if some supreme Governour determined not in matters of worship: For 1. It was not so, when no Supreme Governour determined, on earth: 2. But either you mean the *Substantials* of Gods Worship or the *Circumstantials*: In the first as *faith* is not to be got by force, so neither is *Godliness*, but yet Governours should here do their best: But as to the other we abhor the Conceit, that there are as *many Religions*, as there is difference about *vestures, gestures, days and meats*:

But

But perhaps you take the word *Religion* in the Romane sense, as you confine it to those that you call [*the Religious*] (as if you took the people of your Church to be irreligious:) And so *you* have indeed *too many Religious*, however they come to make one Church.: The Religion of the *Carthusians* is one, and of the *Benedictines* another, and of the *Franciscans* another; I cannot name them all: One eateth Herbs and Fish, and another eateth Flesh seldom, another often; one weareth one habit, and another weareth another; one Religion hath one Rule of Life, and another hath another. But with us there is but *one Religion* (which is the *Christian.*) though one man wear cloth and another stuffe, one white and another black, one eat Flesh and another Fish, and another can seldom get either; though one wear his Hair long and another short, though one be old and another be young, yet we are all of one Religion: Yea, though one preach and pray in English, another in Welch, another in French, and another in Dutch, yet we take not these to be so many Religions: No nor though one think *Free praying* fitter for Ministers than an *imposed Form*, and another think an *imposed Form* only fit, and a third think as the meer Puritan, that *both* having their Conveniences and Inconveniences, there should be seasons *for both*.

And I pray you here tell me two things if you can. 1. Whether the great *difference of Liturgies* (which are the very *words* and *Order* of the *Churches Worship*) be not liker a *difference of Religions*, than the *colour* of our *cloaths*, or the *meat* we *eat*, or the *lighting* of a *Candle*, *&c.* And yet do I need to tell you how many Liturgies are recorded in the *Bibliotheca Patrum*? Yea, that it was six hundred years and more before the Churches in *one Empire* used all one and the same Liturgy? and for some hundred

hundred years, that every Church used what the Bishop pleased? Yea, that the first restraint of *free-praying* that we find was, by a Council ordaining that the Presbyter should first shew his Prayer to the Fathers that they might be sure it was sound? And had *Basil* and *Chrysostome*, and all others that varyed, as divers *Religions* as *Liturgies*?

2. Whether all the *doctrinal* Controversies among your selves, as between all your School *Doctors* about Predestination, Grace, and free will, about Perseverance, about the Immaculate Conception of the Virgin *Mary*, about the Power of the Pope over all Kings in Temporals, and about the killing of excommunicate Kings, and the absolving their Subjects, and whether after excommunication they *are Kings* or *no*, (of which *Hen. Fowlis* hath cited great store on one side,) and all the Moral Controversies about loving God, about Perjuries, Vows, Murder, Fornication, Lying, Stealing, Drunkenness, Gluttony, (of which you may see great store in *Montaltus*'s Letters, The Mystery of Jesuitisme, and Mr. *Clarkson*s late Book called *The Practical Divinity of the Church of Rome:*) I say, is not Religion as much concerned about all these differences, and all the rest among you which make many Horse-loads, yea I think Cart-loads of Volumes, as it is in the colour of the Preachers Cloaths, or the Meat he eateth? And are not Protestants (that is, *meer Christians* disowning Popery) as justifiable in their Unity and Charity, for taking Men to be of the same Religion, who use not the same Garments, Gestures, and Ceremonies, and that bear with differences herein, as your Church that beareth with all these loads of different Doctrines in your most Learned Famous Doctors (and not in the weaker Priests alone) even whether excommunicate

municate Kings may be killed or no; and whether the Pope hath Power to put down and set up Emperours and Kings? If you say that your *One Religion* and *One Church* hath no such difference, it must be by saying that you all agree to *Gregory* the seventh in *Concil. Rom. & Innoc.* 3. in *Concil. Lateran.* on the worser side, and all own the Doctors cited by *H. Fowlis* aforesaid: But indeed I must speak better of you, even that some are of a better mind, whom *Goldastus* hath gathered and preserved, and divers of the Learned Men of *France*, and some in *Spain*. But we think the difference even between the Prelatists, Presbyterians, Independants, yea and the moderate Anabaptists, to be far less than these which your unanimous agreeing Church doth constantly bear with, without Silencing, Imprisoning, Ejecting, or Condemning, or so much as *disowning* the judgments of the worser side.

He that readeth *Parsons* on one side, and *Watson's Quodlibets* on the other; *Barclay* and *Witherington* on one side, and *Zuarez* and the far greater prevalent Party on the other, will either wonder at the *strength of your Unity* which no doctrinal differences even about the Blood of Kings can at all dissolve; or else he may wonder at the laxe and sandie temperament of such Protestants as cannot bear with a Man that readeth not in their Book, and singeth not in their Tune; and is still crying out against others as Sectaries, because they *have piped to them and they have not danced*; and such as no Man can live quietly within reach of, unless they swallow every Morsel which they cut for them, having Throats neither wider, or at least no narrower than theirs. As if King *Henry* the eighth's days were the measure of true Discipline, when one Man was burnt for being too far from Popery, and another hanged, or beheaded, for being

ing Popish, and it was hard to know the middle Region, and harder to know how long it would be calm? till strangers cryed, *Deus bone, quomodo hic vivunt Gentes.* But as none are more cruel in Wars than Cowards, (nor in Robberies than Women,) nor any more gentle and pitiful than valiant experienced Souldiers; so few are so insolent and bloody obtruders of their Dictates and Wills upon the World, as those that being least able to prove them good, have nothing but Inquisitions and Prisons, Silencings and Banishings, Fire and Faggot, effectually to make them good.

But if St. *James* be in the right, who saith, that *Pure Religion and undefiled is this, to visit the Fatherless and Widows in their adversity, and to keep our selves unspotted of the world,* then certainly the *Jesuits Morals,* and the *Mystery of Jesuitism,* and *Clarkson*'s *Roman Practical Divinity,* and *Fowlis*'s Treasons of the Papists, contain more of the concerns of Religion, than preaching in a consecrated or unconsecrated place, and than eating Flesh, Fish, or neither, in *Lent* or on *Fridays,* doth. O the strange difference between your Unity and Concord, and the Protestants! How fast is yours? How loose is ours?

And it is to be considered we pretend not to so much perfection in this world, as ever to expect that all Men should be just of the same Size and Complexion, or speak the same Language, or have all the same Opinions, Thoughts, or Words: If we can keep the *Unity of the Spirit in the Bond of Peace,* in the seven Points named by the Apostle, *Eph.* 4. 3, 4, 5, 6. so far as we have attained do walk by the same Rule (of Love and Peace) and mind the same things, till God reveal more to such as differ, (*Phil.* 3.) we shall be glad of such a measure of Union: For we believe it impossible to be perfect in Concord; while most, yea all are so wofully imperfect in Knowledge, Faith, Love and Obedience. We wait for perfection of all in Heaven; and we find that few things in the World ever did so much against Unity, as pretending to more than is to be hoped for, and laying in on so high terms, and so many as we know will never be received. Therefore our Mutual Love and forbearance with different Forms and Circumstances, is agreeable to the Principles of our Religion.

But for you that pretend to *Unity, Concord, and Infallible Judgement*, to tolerate Cart-loads of Doctrinal Controversies, divers Expositions of many hundred Texts of Scripture, divers readings of the Text it self, contrary Doctrines about God's Grace, about all the Ten Commandments, about the Estates and Lives of Kings, and never so much as to condemn either side nor silence the Preachers, never imprison them, or banish them five miles from Cities and Corporations, never put them to any disgrace, but still honour them as renowned Doctors, as if the Lives of Kings, and the rest of these things were less than a Form of Prayer, or a Ceremony, yea when your Inquisition torment poor Protestants for smaller matters, (as reading the Bible, or a Protestant Book;) methinks all this sheweth that Christian Concord is founded on better Principles than yours, and that yours is but the Bond of your Clergy interest.

CHAP.

CHAP. IV.

His own false Description of Papists.

YOUR next work being to give your Relations, first the *false* and then the *true* description of a *Papist*, it's most deceitful work that you make in both.

I. In the false description you do quite pass over the great *Constitutive* Causes of Popery, in which it is that it differs from *Apostolical Christianity*: And you name a few of the superstructures or remoter differences, and cite not one Protestant that speaketh those words, but only the present *Arch-bishop of York*, and as you say, the *vulgar* conceit: And you are ordinarily careful, in every Paragraph, to put in *some one word*, by the disowning of which you may disown the sentence.

But, 1. Is it not a meer deceiving trick to word your own Accusations so in the Protestants name, as you know you can easilyest plead, *Not Guilty*? May not one alter some *one word* in every Verse of any Chapter in the Bible, and then protest, that *not one of all those Verses is in the Bible*? So if the Printer have some *Errata* in each Leaf of your Book, may you not protest that not one Leaf of it is yours?

2. And is it not deceitfully done to appeal to the *Vulgar* as the Accusers, that thus charge you, when you know how vain it is to expect, that, (how sound soever their judgments be) the Vulgar should state any Controversies so exactly, as not to miss it in a *word*, or *more*, when they hit the sense. And you knew how hard it is to disprove you: For who shall judge what is the opinion of

of the Vulgar? If I should say that *few* or *none* of my acquaintance do charge you to speak those very words, you may say that *you know some that do*, and I cannot confute you.

3. And have you not the Differences between you and us voluminously stated and handled long ago, by many whose Books have been received by the Churches, and Licensed by Authority, when the *Vulgar stating* of them was never Licensed nor owned? Why did you not gather out of *Jewel*, *Usher's Answer* to the *Jesuites Challenge*, Dr. *Challoner*, *Chillingworth*, Dr. *Field*, Dr. *Crakenthorp*, Dr. *Reignolds*, Dr. *John White*, Bishop *Morton*, Dr. *Ames*, *Sadeel*, *Chamier*, *Whitakers*, or such others, what the things are that Protestants charge you with? And answer what is there charged on you?

I my self have enumerated many of the things which we take for Popery, and not to be defended, in my *Key for Catholicks*, and in my *Safe Religion*, and in One *Sheet against Popery*, almost twenty years ago; and since then in my [*Full and easie satisfaction which is the true Religion*,] and in my [*Certainty of Christianity without Popery*.] And you have given no answer to any one of them that I ever heard of: But you can better dispute, it seems, with your *Relations*, and with the *Women* and *Country-Labourers*, or *Tradesmen*, that never use to speak in that strictness of words as shall prevent the Cavils of a studied Sophister.

4. As for the A. B. of *York*, I am almost a Stranger to him; and more to his Book, which I never saw: But two things I can say, 1. That we are no more obliged to justifie his words, than you to justifie the words of any one of your Doctors. 2. That no man is so fit to answer for him as he is for himself. Because no man knoweth so
well

well in what sense he took the word [*Papist*.] I suppose you know that *Grotius*, who perswadeth us all to an *obedient Union with your Church, under the Popes Government according to the Canons, owning the Decrees of all the Councils, even that of* Trent, yet for all this doth speak against *Papists*: But he tells you that by *Papists* he meaneth *those Flatterers of the Pope, who approve of all that he saith or doth*. And that it was not the *Government* or *Doctrine* of that Church that was to have been *reformed*, but the *Opinions* of some *Schoolmen*, and the *excesses*, and *ill lives* of *many* of the *Clergie*. Now could not *Grotius* easily have produced such *Papists* as these, as having said as gross things as you recite?

And how far Bishop *Bromhall*, and the Doctor that lately published him, own *Grotius*, I will not tell you, but refer you to their own words: To which many more might easily be added. Now suppose that Dr. *Heylin*, or A. Bishop *Bromhall*, or his Prefacer should say, that by [*Papists*] they mean such as *Grotius* did, do you think that they could not prove as gross words, as any cited by you, in some such Flatterers of the Pope? And you know, I suppose, that some of late would not have the *Church of Rome* called *Papists*, or at least so charged, but only the *Court of Rome*.

But let us take notice of some of the Particulars.

I. Your first Article is, That *Papists are said to Worship Stocks and Stones, Medals, and Pictures of Jesus Christ as Gods, and pray to them, and put their whole confidence in them, as the ancient Heathens did in their dumb Idols of* Jupiter, Mars, *&c.*

Ans. 1. Your Doctors are oft charged with maintaining that the Image of *Christ* and the *Cross* must be *worshipped with latria*, which is the Worship called Divine:

And

And instead of this you put in the word [*is Gods.*] It is not [*as reputing these Images to be really Gods,*] but [*worshipping them as God only should be worshipped,*] contrary to the second Commandment, which forbiddeth such *Bodily actions* as were symbolical of Idol-Worship, though the *Mind* were kept never so free from accounting God to be like Idols, or Idols to be Gods.

2. Who chargeth you of putting your *whole trust in Images?* Is not *part of it* too much?

3. How prove you that the Heathens ordinarily did so? Or that they took *Jupiter, &c.* to be nothing but *the Image*, and not a *Cœlestial Power?*

4. But instead of saying any more on this point, I again tell you, that Dr. *Stillingfleet* hath in his new Defence against *T. G.* so fully proved that the generality of the Heathen Nations did worship one Universal Supreme God, and worshipped their inferior Gods much like as you do Angels, and worshipped their Images, not as being Gods themselves, but with such a Relation to the Deity, as you do your Images; and that your Image Worship is such as the ancient Fathers condemned in the Heathens; that none of you will ever be able solidly to confute him, or defend your Idols any more: So dear do you pay for *T. G.* his temporary triumph.

II. Your second feigned Charge is, [*That the Pope can give men leave to commit any sin for money---or so pardon any sin after, as you shall not be in the least danger of any punishment for it temporal, or eternal, in Purgatory, or in Hell.*]

Ans. I will take your part in this, and prove that the Squib-maker, who drew up this Charge, doth do you wrong. What a Sot was he to think that any Pope would ever be sick, or sore, or dye, if he could forgive

all

all temporal punishment? Unless the unhappy man can forgive all others, and not himself? At least he would preserve some of his Friends in health and immortality on Earth? And the Whores, that *Baronius* himself saith made Popes at their pleasure, would have found some Popes so grateful as to have saved them from dying, if not from bringing forth in pain. And truly I should hope that at least the Pope that by a Council was condemned for an Infidel, and believing not any life to come in Heaven or Hell, would have been so tender-hearted as to forgive all the world the punishment in Hell. And it was a great mistake in these Slanderers of you, to except no sin: As if the Popes could forgive them that would diminish their Kingdoms, or restrain their Domination; much less that would depose them. Could Pope *Eugenius* ever forgive the Universal Church, as it's called, that is, the great General Council which in vain condemned and deposed him? When he can scarce forgive a poor Protestant the Rack and Fire, for reading the Bible or serving God out of the *Roman* way.

And doubtless he is wronged by this Charge, that he can nullifie all *pain, death, Purgatory, and Hell*; for I think you will say, that *quoad potentiam ordinatam* Christ cannot do it, or at least he will not. And were this believed by all the World, no wonder if they willingly obeyed him, and called him, *Our Lord God the Pope*. For he could conquer any Kingdom, by saving all his Souldiers from hurt and death.

It is enough that he can forgive some *part* or *time* of Purgatory Torments, and that (as great Doctors say) he can (and lesser Priests than he) forgive the pains of Hell to a sinner that hath no true *contrition* for sin (that is, repenteth not out of any Love to God or Goodness)

L   but

but only *Attrition* and the *Sacrament of Penance and Absolution*, (that is, repenteth only for fear of Hell, and would sin still if he durst.)

And though you may hope that there are no Copies of the old Pardons yet to be seen, or any of *Tecelius* Merchandise now extant, yet the sure History of them is common, and if you deny it, it will be proved to your shame. What a multitude of Writers have better cited your practice and confuted it?

But yet I remember (to do you right) that even *Hildebrand* himself (*Greg. 7.*) in a *Roman* Council saith, that [*neither the Sacrament of Baptism, nor Penance is of any force to pardon any impenitent Hypocrite,*] which is well said; and as for true *Penitent Believers*, we verily believe that they are pardoned *ipso jure* by the Gospel, as to destructive or hellish Punishment; and that every true Minister of Christ may validly deliver this pardon ministerially, by true absolution, in the Sacrament, and without it. But in what *measure* God himself will remit *temporal Chastisements*, few men can know till the event tell it them: And neither Pope nor Priest can forgive without him; nor know what God will remit, any more than another man may know, that is, by Gods Word, and by the event.

And again, I say if it were in the Popes power (however you may absolve him from Bribery or the Love of Money) that there would be more difference in point of bodily suffering, between his Subjects or Favourites and other men, than was ever yet perceived. It's policy therefore to confine the business to *Purgatory*, that no witness may be able to disprove it.

You add to the Charge, [*That of all Christ's Merits the Pope is the Supreme Lord, to dispose of them to the living*

living and the dead, as he by his unerring Spirit thinks fitting.]

Answ. Here the Charger wrongs you too: For seeing all mens Lives and Mercies are the Fruits of Christs *Merits*, if this were true, the Pope could kill all his Enemies at his pleasure, and when he hath killed them could cast them into Hell, or keep them out of Heaven: And then no one in his wits would be against him, or displease him. It's enough to be able to do as aforesaid.

III. Your next is [*the Papist honours the Virgin Mary much more than he does her divine Son, or God the Father: for one Prayer he says to God, he says ten to the Virgin.*]

Answ. This is injurious too, whoever made it: The Pagans honour not their Inferiour Gods, so much as the Supreme! And for the *number* of Prayers, it's not like that all Papists use the same, or by the same Beads: But whether you give *inordinate honour* to the Virgin *Mary*, and put not up a very large proportion of your Prayers to her; if Dr. *Stillingfleet*, and abundance before him, may not be trusted in their Citations, I hope your own Prayer-books may be believed. It's bad enough to make her like *Juno*, though you should not equal her with *Jove*. Angels have refused smaller honour.

IV. You add [*His Prayers are a company of Latine words, he neither understands, or cares to understand them, which if he do but patter over in such a number, though his heart and mind be wholly taken up with worldly thoughts and desires, he thinks,* &c.]

Answ. At the first line one would have thought you had grown past blushing, and had *denyed* your *Latine Prayers*, not understood; but you never want *one word* to help you out in renouncing the whole Sentence: You make me think of that sorry Religion which teacheth

men,

men, that if *one Article in a Vow*, among many, be unlawful, they may renounce all Obligation to any thing else that there is Vowed; and so a Knave may be disobliged to all Vows and Covenants, if he will but drop in any thing that is unlawful. Do not your unlearned Multitude join in your *Latine Prayers*? Do Mass-books, and your daily Masses, all deceive our Eyes and Ears? No, that's not it; what then! must all be *desirous* to understand it, if they cannot? I rather think the Calumny is, that [*his mind and heart may be wholly taken up with worldly desires?*] But who was it that put in that into the Charge? was it not your self? We know that you say, *There should be some General kind of Devotion and good Desire, though he know not what is said*; and *a General Belief*, called *Implicite*, which is *no Belief of any of the Particulars*, and a *General Implicite Desire*, which is *no Desire of any express Particular*, being *a Faith* that is *no Faith*, and *a Prayer* which is *no Prayer*, would make a Religion which is no Religion, if you had no better.

V. The next is [*If he do but believe as his Church-men believe, though he be wholly ignorant of their Belief, his Soul is safe enough.*]

Answ. What is a Man but his Wit? The Word (*wholly*) craftily put in by your self, enableth you also to renounce this Charge: For we all confess that your Doctors commonly hold, that this one Article must be believed, [*That the Church is to be believed and obeyed,*] and that's one Particular. . But I pray tell us if you can:
1. Dare your Church say that every word revealed must be believed Explicitely of necessity to Salvation? No:
2. And have they in any General Council determined what those Particular Articles are that are so necessary, (since you departed from the sufficiency of the Creed?)

Or

Or do not your Doctors, without any Decree of the Church, use to debate it as a free opinion? 3. And do they not differ among themselves, as all in pieces about the Point? And do not your chief Learned School-men cited at large by *Fr. a Sancta Clara* on our Articles hold that the Particular Belief of Christ himself, or the supernatural Articles of the Creed are not of necessity? And I know not of any one thing that you are agreed to be necessary, besides the Belief that the *Church*, (that is, the *Pope and his Council*) *are Infallible*, or to be believed and obeyed; and it is a Learned School Doctor and Jesuite *Fran. Albertinus Corol. p.* 250. that justifieth a Countryman that should believe a falshood if twenty Bishops tell it him, and that the Command of Faith doth oblige to believe falshood, it being *not per se, but per accidens, &c.* And I think the old man is now among you at *London*, (*Fr. a Sancta Clara*,) who having cited abundance of Doctors against the necessity of believing in Christ or any Supernatural Point, or in some cases knowing the Law of Nature and the Decalogue, saith p. 20. [*To speak my sence freely, I think that the Common People committing themselves to the instruction of the Pastors, trusting their knowledge and goodness, if they be deceived, it shall be accounted invincible ignorance, or probable at least:* So Herera; *which excuseth from fault: Yea, some Doctors give so much to the Instruction of Doctors on whom the care of the Flock lyeth, that if they teach* hic & nunc *that God would be hated, that a rude Parishioner is bound to believe them.* See abundance more in him cited, Deus, Nat. Grat. Probl. 15, and 16. And that you may know that this opinion is not rare, he addeth, *p.* 123. [*It seemeth to be the common opinion of the Schools and Doctors at this day, that the Laity erring with their Tea-*

chers,

chers, or *Pastors*, are altogether excused from all fault: Yea, by erring thus many wayes materially they merit for the Act of Christian Obedience which they owe their Teachers, *as* Valentia *faith* To. 3. Disp. 1. q. 2. p. 5. *and others with* Angles, Vas. quez. *&c.*]

And if this be true, what Prince, Lord, or any other Lay-man, that would be out of all danger of Sin and Hell, would not be a Papist, and be sure to chuse a Priest that is ignorant enough to take Perjury, Drunkenness, Gluttony, Adultery, Fornication, Persecution, Opression for no Sin, and then he may be sure that it's none to him, but he meriteth by obeying him that will perswade him to it?

And what if these bid Subjects kill their Kings, would it not be sinless and meritorious by this Rule?

But you'll say, These be but the words of Writers, and Books may be misunderstood, when they say that this is the common Opinion of the Doctors. And perhaps if I talk with you, or another, you will protest that this is none of your belief. But how shall I know that *W. H.* or his Neighbour, or Grandfather, know better what is the Faith or Religion of the Papists than the old Queens Confessor, and all those famous Doctors, whom he citeth, and all that I my self have read?

And remember your Undertaking, cited in my Title Page.

Is it not the most common Opinion of your Doctors, that all men are bound to know and believe according to their opportunities, and probable instructions? But what is commonly necessary your Learned Church-men cannot tell us, no not the Pope or Councils? And who can tell what other mens capacities and opportunities have been? and so whether he be a Believer indeed, or not? or bound to be so? VI. Your

VI. Your next part is, [*He makes Gods of -- sinful men :* — *He maketh less scruple of violating Gods Laws, than he doth any Ordinance of the Pope, or any Law of his Church.*]

Ans. That one word [*any*] is either the falshood of your Accuser, or the *craft* of the Clark that drew up the Inditement: And I think it should not be drawn up of these Laws compared *formaliter*, but *materialiter*: For I cannot think you so unreasonable, as to think that the Pope is above God; but that when you cast away God's Laws to keep the Pope's, it is because you think that the Pope hath power to change and abrogate God's Laws, or dispense with them; or that you are bound to believe that it is none of Gods Law, if the Pope say it's none: For Instance, 1. I know that you cast away Christ's Law for receiving his Body and Blood, the Cup as well as the Bread in the Sacrament: But *why* you do so, I am no Judge.

2. I know that you break the Second Commandment, and usually leave it out of the Decalogue too: But why you do it, I am no Judge.

3. I know that the Pope and his approved General Council at *Laterane* make a Law against Gods Law for obedience to the higher powers, and this Papists profess to receive as part of their Religion: But on what reasons you do it, I leave to you.

You Instance [*If he commit Fornication it is but a Venial Sin*] Do You hold that any of your approved Councils have defined it to be a Mortal Sin? If so, I hope you will take those for Heretical that think it is not always so: I refer you to Mr. *Clarksons Practical Divinity* aforesaid, and the Jesuites Morals. But doubtless all of you have not the same Judgment either of Fornication or Murder, (as is there proved;) for you are not bound to to be so far agreed, in such little things: But your craft put in the *saving word* next, [*and sprinkling himself with a little Holy Water he is as free from all spot as a new Baptized Infant.*]

Answ. They say, *No Man wrongeth himself:* You may lay a false Charge against your self that you may the easier deny it; There must be somewhat more than *Holy water*, else what need of *Attrition* and Confession, and Penance, if it please the Priest, or Commutation of Penance? what need the Crusado's to have killed so many thousands of the *Waldenses* and *Albigenses* to procure the pardon of their sins. (O dreadful way to pardon!) What room for Pilgrimages, satisfactions, or for Purgatory, or for Masses to be said for the Souls in Purgatory, or for praying to the Virgin *Mary*, and abundance such, if *Holy Water alone* would do all the Business? Was not he much overseen, or did grosly prevaricate, that drew up this Charge? Might I but chuse my Adversaries Advocate, and agree with him to say nothing but what I can disprove, I would certainly have the better, and be justified.

VII. The next part is, [*And as for his obedience to Magistrates, if they be not of his Religion, he owes them no allegiance: And if he have by Oath obliged himself, he has a holy Father can dispense with him for that, or any other Oath, for a piece of Money: If his Prince persecute him for his Religion, let him but have so much desperate courage as to sacrifice his own life to stab or poyson his said Persecutor, he shall at Rome be canonized for a Saint: Nor can private Persons expect any fidelity from him, when he is thus traiterously rebellious against his Liege Lord and Soveraign,* &c.]

Ans. Now I perceive you are over bold, and do too hardly

hardly blush, when you have the face to bring in such an instance, and by the inserting of a word or two of your own, to dare to wash off from your Religion the blot of Perfidiousness and Rebellion, when it is part of the Decrees of your approved General Council. The Prevaricator wrongeth you, 1. By making [*not of his Religion*] to be all that's necessary to free you from allegiance. 2. By putting in [*or any other Oath for a piece of Money:*] I have not yet found that the Pope undertaketh to dispense with a man that will swear to *believe the Roman Church*, or the rest in Pope *Pius* his *Trent* Oath, nor yet with the Vow of Baptism, if seconded by an Oath. 3. By saying only [*If his Prince persecute him;*] for the Doctors say that he must be first *excommunicate*, or a Heretick at least, and some say he must have the Pope's Order before he may kill a King; and the Council only speaketh of *Deposing*, and not of killing. 4. And the Prevaricator too rashly promised [*Canonizing:*] He that murdered one of the *French* Kings, was but *praised* in an Oration by the Pope, (proved by many) but not Canonized: *Garnet* was not every one.

But because I see you grow so bold, (and also in what follows return to what you had said before) I will, instead of following you farther, tell you what such as I mean by a *Papist*, and what some other men mean by him.

M CHAP.

CHAP. V.

The true History of the Papacy, its original and growth.

Though I reserve the opening of the ambiguities of the word *Papist* till near the end, I shall so far anticipate that, as to tell you here also, that the word [PAPIST] is equivocal: I. In the sense of *Grotius*, and all our Reverend Country-men that are of his judgment, [" *Papists are those that without any difference do approve of all the sayings and doings of Popes, for honour or lucre sake as is usual,*] Discus. p. 15.

If of all, then of all the Adulteries, Murders, Simonie, Heresie, Infidelity charged on some of them by their own Writers and by Councils. I am sorry if this be [*usual*] I hope yet that there are few of these Papists in the World, and that few Popes themselves will deny that they are sinners.

But he elsewhere desireth the Reformation, 1. Of some bold disputes of the School-men; 2. And the ill lives of the Clergie; 3. And some Customs which have neither Councils, nor Tradition.

II. Some who are for the Supremacy of *General Councils* above the Pope, do call those *Papists* that are for the *Pope's Supremacy above such Councils*; or that give him the Legislative as well as the Judicial Power over the Universal Church: Though themselves give him the Supreme Judicial Power when there is no General Council.

III. Protestants call those Papists who hold that the
Roman

Roman Pope is rightfully the Governour of the Universal Church on Earth, either as to Legislative or Judicial-executive Power, either with Councils or without. Two things are here included in our Judgment. 1. *That there is no rightful Universal Governour under Christ over all the Church on Earth,* either as to *Legislation,* or *Judgment:* 2. That the *Roman Pope therefore is no such Governour.*

In this third sense now I am to tell you what we Protestants mean by a *Papist* more particularly. And first I must tell you what a *POPE* is, before I can well tell you what a Papist is: Which I shall do, I. *De facto Historically:* II. *De jure* as to the *Power* which he *claimeth.*

I. A long time the Bishops of *Rome* were seldome called *Popes,* and other Bishops were so called as well as they: At first the Bishops of *Rome* were pious persecuted Men, and many of them Martyrs, and usurped no Power over any Churches but their own; which with *Alexandria* were the two first that brake *Ignatius* his Test of Unity, who saith, [*To every Church there is one Altar, and one Bishop with his fellow Presbyter and Deacons.*] But *Rome* having long called her self the Mistris of the World, and being the Seat of the Empire and Senate, and of the Governing Power of the *orbis Romanus,* the Christians there grew greater than others, and the Bishop as it increased kept it under his Power: And when Christians had peace (which was under the far greatest part of the Heathen Emperours, and for the far longest time) the Greatness of *Rome* giving Greatness to that Church, and so to the Bishop, and great opportunity to help other Churches, because the Governing Power of the Empire was there, this Bishop grew to be of *greatest wealth* and *interest*: And in times of Peace the Strife which Christ

M 2 once

once ended was taken up among the Bishops [*which of them should be the greatest* :] And St. *Paul* having taught Christians that they should not *go voluntarily to Law against each other before Heathens*, if there were but *a wise man among them to be an Arbitrator* ; the Christians supposing that they had none wiser or fitter than their Bishop, made him their Common *Arbitrator* in things Civil, as well as Ecclesiastical: By which means Custom making it like a Law, Bishops became *de facto Church-Magistrates*: But they had no Power to execute any *Penal Laws*, either *Jewish* or *Roman*, or to make any of their own, except as Arbitrators or Doctors to those that would voluntarily receive them: And they had no Power of Life and Death, nor to dis-member any, nor to beat or scourge them, nor to Fine them or Confiscate their Estates: But being entrusted by *Christ* as his Ministers with the Power of the *Church-Keys*, and by the *People* with the Power of *Civil Arbitrations*, they were by this the *stated Governours of all Christians* ; who yet obeyed the *Roman* Heathen Magistrates, but brought none of their own differences voluntarily before them.

And because that Multitudes of Heresies took advantage of the Churches liberty, and swarmed among them to their great weakning and disgrace, and christ had commanded his Servants to serve him in as much *Unity* and *Concord* as they could, duty and necessity drove the Pastors of the Churches to *Correspondencies*, and to *meet together* on all just occasions, and at last to *Associations* for the ordering of these Meetings! In which they agreed in what *Compass* and in what *Place*, or by *whose Call* such Meetings should be held, and what Bishops in those Meetings should *preside* or sit highest, and first speak and subscribe: And usually they thought that to follow the

Order

Order of the Civil Government, and give precedency to thoſe that were Biſhops of ſuch Cities as had precedency in the Civil Government, was the moſt convenient Order: And in theſe Meetings they agreed on ſuch Canons or Orders for all in that Compaſs to obſerve, as they thought beſt tended to their ends: And having no forcing Power (as is aforeſaid) they formed their Impoſitions on voluntarily penitents ſo as might ſerve inſtead of the Power of the Sword: Even Murderers, Inceſtuous, Adulterers, they could not puniſh with Death, Stripes, or Mulcts; and they were loth to diſgrace Chriſtianity ſo much as to accuſe ſuch to the Heathen Magiſtrates; and therefore they laid the greater ſhame upon them, forbidding them Communion with Chriſtians for ſo many years as they thought meet, and before they reſtored them they were humbly to beg the Prayers and Communion of the Church. But yet theſe Synods were ſmall and few and rare, and never any dreamt of them as a Council of all the Church on Earth.

But when God bleſſed the *Rome* World with a Chriſtian Emperour after the ſharp Perſecution of *Dioclefian*, and this Emperour had by Religion and Intereſt made the *Chriſtian Souldiers* his *chief confidents* or *ſtrength*, he ſtudied the utmoſt *increaſe of the Chriſtians*, and to that end invited all to Chriſtianity, by the favour of the Court, and by ſuch Honours, Commands, Wealth, and Dignities, as they were capable of; and above all he exalted the Chriſtian Biſhops, whom he *found* the Rulers of the Chriſtian Societies: He gave them Honours, and Wealth, and Power: He made a Law that no Chriſtians ſhould be forced to go to the Civil Heathen Judicatures, from their Biſhops, and gave Power to the Biſhops to be the Chriſtians Judges, ſome few hainous Crimes being in time excepted:

excepted: And so the Bishops were by *his Law* made *Civil Magistrates* or *Arbitrators*; yet not with any Power of Life, or Limbs, or Estate: So that all that would become Christians, and would be subject to the Bishops Canons, and Church Discipline, were freed from Death, Stripes, and Mulcts, for many Crimes which all others were lyable to, and Excommunication and some Penance was instead of all: By such means Multitudes of worldly Men, and by the Preaching of the Gospel Multitudes that were sound Christians, came together into the Churches: And Bishopricks being now very desirable for their Power, Honour, and Wealth, Men that most loved *Power, Honour,* and *Wealth,* (that is, *Proud, Worldly, Carnal Men*) did earnestly seek them, and strive for Precedency in them: But yet while the People had the choice, or a Negative therein, and the old Spirit of Christianity remained in many of the Bishops, in many places bad ones were kept out, and many excellent Men were preferred.

The Heresie of *Arrius* and the *Alexandrian* Contentions thereabout, required a remedy for the Churches Peace: The Bishops could not end it themselves: It spread so far that it was *Constantine*'s great grief to see Christians so quickly disgrace themselves, and weaken their Religion in the Eyes of the Heathens: Therefore he called a Council of Bishops consisting mostly of those of the Eastern parts where the troubles arose: Two Priests of *Rome* were there, but not the Bishop, nor but few of the West: Where the Emperours open Rebukes and Lamentation for their Contention, and his earnest Exhortation to Peace, and his burning all the Libells or Accusations which the Bishops brought in against each other, and his continual presence and moderating oversight

sight of them, brought that meeting at last to that good and peaceable End, which else it was never like to have attained.

It never came into *Constantine*'s mind to call this Council as an Universal Representative of the whole Christian World, or as the Governours of the Churches that were out of his Dominions; but as a fit expedient to end the strife that was raised in those Parts: For as few of the West were there, so none of all other Kingdoms were once called. For who should call them? *Constantine* that called the Council neither did it, nor ever pretended to a power to do it. The Pope called not the Council, much less did he call the rest of the Christian World: *Socrates* tells us, *l.* 1. *c.* 15. that St. *Thomas* had Preached to the *Parthians*, and *Bartholomew* to the *Indians*, and *Matthew* to the *Ethiopians*, though the middle *India* was not Converted till *Constantine*'s days, by *Frumentius*, and *Edesius*, and *Iberia* by a Maid:] And so *Euseb. l.* 3. *c.* 3. who saith, that St. *Andrew* Preached to the *Scythians*; and *in Vit. Constant. l.* 4. *c.* 8. that there were many Churches in *Persia*: And no doubt these Apostles Preached not in vain: *Scotland* and other Countries that were out of the *Roman* Empire had Churches. Yet any Neighbour Bishop that desired it, might voluntarily be present. When *Theodoret* (in his Life) tells us that [*James* Bishop of *Nisibis* (in the borders of *Persia*) was at the Council of Nice: For Nisibis was then under the Government of the Roman Empire,] he plainly intimateth that none but the Subjects of the Empire were called: And the names yet visible, of the Subscribers prove it.

Notwithstanding this Councils decisions, the Contentions continue, and the Major part of the Bishops went

went that way usually as the Emperours went: And so in the Reign of *Constantius*, and *Valens*, they most turned to the *Arrians*, at least in words: And many General Councils (so called, of the Empire) the *Arrians* had, in which they prevailed, and made Creeds for their turn as they at *Nice* had done against them, and brought Persecution on the Orthodox, silencing, and ejecting them, and scattering their Meetings as prohibited Conventicles, the Emperour himself sometime executing their dispersions and restraint: And among other *Liberius* the Bishop of *Rome*, against his Conscience Subscribed to them.

The Fathers at the Council of *Nice* did determine of the bounds of the Patriarchs of the Empire, which being at first but three, (*Rome*, *Alexandria*, and *Antioch*,) *Jerusalem* was after added, and after that *Constantinople*: For *Constantine* having now strengthned himself by the Christian Interest, and being further out of the danger of mutable Souldiers, than his Predecessours, did that which none of them was ever able to do, by removing the Imperial Seat from *Rome* to *Constantinople*, and so leaving that Famous City as naked and almost neglected: Whereby two great changes befell the Clergie, 1. The Bishop of *Rome* was left more absolute and uncontrouled in the West; 2. And the Bishop of *Constantinople* set up against him for the *Primacy* in the Empire: At first he claimed but an *Equality*, but afterward a *Priority as Universal Bishop*, because his Seat was the Imperial Seat.

The Patriarch of *Jerusalem* was so far from the Court, and of so small power, that he made the least stir of any of the five, though he had the fairest pretense incomparably for a claim of Supremacy on Religious reasons, if a *Supreme* there must have been (*Christ* himself having been there a *Minister to the Circumcision*, and Shepherd of of the Sheep of the House of *Israel*, and his Kinsman *James* then Bishop after, and that being the *Mother-Church* out of which sprung all the rest.) But the other four Patriarchs (especially three of them) became as so many *Generals of Armies* militating frequently against each other: and he that got the *stronger* Party of Bishops and Court-favourers carryed all, against the rest. But no place more turbulent, nor no Bishop more unquiet than those of *Alexandria*: Pride and Worldliness now grew apace, and so corrupted the Clergie, that in their Synods the *fleshly* part too oft prevailed against the *spiritual*! When Court and Councils were for the *Arrians*, the whole Eastern part of the Empire was embroiled in the Contention, and the Orthodox in the greater Bishopricks cast out: When they were down and cast out themselves, the temporizing and turbulent Bishops usually got the Major Vote: Excellent *Gregory Nazianzen* for the great service that he had done against the *Arrians* was chosen by the People, and made Patriarch of *Constantinople*: But the Synod of Bishops envyed him and rejected him, to whom he gave place and would not strive. *Dioscorus* of *Alexandria* and his party fought it out at the General Council, and killed *Flavianus*: And being after overcome and outed of his Seat, did still claim and keep the Title with his followers, and the most of his Patriarchate of the People stuck to him; so that he propagated his Opinion and Interest in all those remote parts of the Empire: Yea among Volunteers in *Ethiopia* and other *extra*-imperial parts, which no Law or Canon had subjected to him; while the Patriarch that succeeded him by the Councils Decree, had his party only as the rest, *within the Empire*: So that to this day the *Syrians*, *Ethiopians*, and abundance others profess themselves the

follow-

followers of *Dioscorus* as the true Bishop injuriously, say they, cast out.

Chrysostome afterwards was cast out of his Patriarchate of *Constantinople*, by a Synod of Bishops and the Court.

At *Rome* the Bishoprick was such a prey, that contending for it troubled the Publick Peace: At the choice of *Damasus* they fought it out in the Church, and his party won that sacred Field, leaving many Carcasses there to the Church-Communion of the dead.

But it became the great advantage of *Rome*, that when the Empire was divided, the Western Emperour proved Orthodox while the Eastern were oft *Arrians*: Which kept up the honour of the Western Bishops who had not the temptations of the East; where sharp persecutions and the desolation of their Flocks, and the boast of the *Arrians* as the Major part, that was also setled by Authority, caused the ejected Bishops sometime to solicite them of the West for help, by sending them some to acquaint the *Arrians* that their Cause was owned by the Western Bishops, or to put some Countenance on their depressed Cause (and indeed the Western Emperour did rescue them.) This occasioneth the Papists to this day to pretend that this was an Act of their subjection to the Pope: St. *Basil* was the chief in this solicitation, and you shall read his words (Translated.)

"*Verily the manners of proud men* (speaking of the
"Western Bishops) *use to grow more insolent, if they be
"honoured: And if God be merciful to us, what other ad-
"dition have we need of? but if Gods anger remain on us,
"what help can the pride of the West bring us? when they
"neither know the truth, nor can endure to speak it ; but
"being prepossessed with false suspicions they do the same
"things now which they did in the Case of* Marcellus, *con-*
"*tentiously*

" *tentiously disputing against those that taught the truth,*
" *but for Heresie confirming it by their Authority?* Indeed I
" was willing, (*not as representing the Publick Person of*
" *the East*) *to write to their Leader* (Damasus) *but not*
" *about Church-matters; but that I might intimate that*
" *they neither knew the truth of the things that are done*
" *with us, nor did admit the way by which they might learn*
" *them. And in general, that they should not insult over*
" *the calamitous and afflicted; nor think that Pride did*
" *make for their dignity, when that one sin alone is enough*
" *to make us hateful to God.* But this Epistle of *Basil*
Andr. Schottus the Jesuite left out of *Basil's* Works when
he published them, *Antw. Lat. A. D.* 1616. *Tertullian* had made as bold with the Bishop of *Rome* long before, *lib. de Pudic. pag.* 742. against *Zepherinus:* So had *Cyprian* and *Firmilian* against *Stephen: Hilary Pictav.* with *Liberius* and the Councils, even that of *Nice:* But most notable was the sharp Contest of the *Carthage* Council, of which *Augustine* was one, against *Zosimus,* and *Boniface* and *Celestine*; when the Pope falsly alledged a Canon of the *Nicene* Council for Appeal to *Rome,* they denyed his claim, and evinced the forgery, and stood it out against him to the last.

I. And here you may see that they took not the Pope's Power to be of God (*jure divino:*) For they searched only all the Archives to find out the *true Copies of the Nicene Council,* (*Pisanus* Canons being not then made;) and did not go to the *Scripture* to decide the Case, nor to *Tradition Apostolical,* only pleading *Church-Laws* and Order as on their side.

And that they never dreamt of a *Divine Institution* of this *Roman* Papacy or Primacy, but only as the Arch-Bishop of *Canterbury* in *England* hath precedency by the King's

King's Laws, and not by God's; so *Rome* was the first Seat by the meer appointment of man, even Emperours and Councils, is yet fully evident; 1. In that the *same Power* that made the other *four Patriarchs*, made the Bishop of *Rome* a Patriarch; and he was not made Pope or *Prime Patriarch* before he was made *Patriarch*: But no man dreameth of a Divine Institution of the *other four* Patriarchs: *Ergo*.

2. Because the whole Eastern Church, which was far greater than the Western, first equalled the Patriarch of *Constantinople* to him of *Rome*, and after preferred him; when yet they never dreamed of a Divine Institution of the Patriarchate of *Constantinople*: For it was but lately made: And no man of reason can judge, that all the Catholick Emperours, Bishops, and People of the far greatest part of the Imperial Church, would professedly equal or prefer a *Humane* Office before one which they believed to be of *Divine* Institution.

3. To this day all the *Greek* Church shew themselves to be of that judgment, by adhering to the Patriarch of *Constantinople*, whom they confess to have been made such by Emperours and Councils. And in the Contest with them the case is commonly pleaded accordingly.

4. *Gregory Nazianzen* would never have wished so earnestly that there were no *inequality*, *superiority*, or *priority of Seats*, if he had taken them to be of Divine Institution: Durst he have so opposed the Law and Order of God?

5. But to put all out of doubt, it is expresly determined by the most famous General Councils, even two of the four which are likened to the four Gospels, *Constantinople* and *Calcedon*, that the Primacy was given to *Rome* by the *Fathers* (so they called Councils) *because it*

was

was the Imperial Seat; and therefore they give *equal* Priviledges to *Constantinople*, because it is the Imperial Seat. The words of the Council of *Calcedon* (oft cited) are these (translated.)

Act. 16. Binii pag. 134. [" *we following always the definitions of the holy Fathers and the Canons, and knowing those that have now been read of the* 150 *Bishops most beloved of God, that were congregated under the Emperour, of pious memory,* Theodosius *the Greater, in the Royal City of* Constantinople, *New* Rome, *have our selves also defined the same things, concerning the Priviledges of the same most holy Church of* Constantinople, *New* Rome: *For to the Seat of old* Rome, *because of the Empire of that City, the Fathers consequently gave the Priviledges. And the* 150 *Bishops most beloved of God, being moved with the same intentions, have given equal Priviledges to the most holy Seat of New* Rome; *reasonably judging that the City adorned with the Empire and Senate, shall enjoy equal Priviledges with old Regal* Rome.

This *Council* was called by the Emperour *Martian*; and his Lay-Officers were called the Judges: And the Bishops, to shew what they thought of *Rome*, cryed out [*They that contradict it are Nestorians: Let them that contradict it walk to* Rome. *Bin. p.* 98.]

If such a General Council *be not to be believed*, farewell all the Papists Infallibility, Authority, Tradition, and Religion: If it *be to be believed*, the Pope is a Humane Creature, and not a Divine.

But *Binius* saith, that *Rome receiveth not the Canons of this Council of Constantinople*, which this confirmeth, but only their condemnation of Macedonius: And he saith [*That every Council hath just so much strength and authority*

rity as the Apostolick See bestoweth on it: For (saith he) *unless this be admitted, no reason can be given why some Councils of greater numbers of Bishops were reprobated, and others of a smaller number confirmed,*] Vol. 2. p. 515. And yet must we hear the noise of [*all the Christian World, and all the Bishops, and General Councils, and the Tradition of our Fore-fathers, &c.*] as against us, when all is but the *Pope of Rome, and such as please him*? and it is *He* and his *Pleasers* that refuse the most General Councils and Tradition? Away with this false deceitful talk.

6. Once more hear their own Confession; Their late English Bishop (of *Calcedon*, a fatal name) *R. Smyth* in his Survey against Bishop *Bromhall* saith, *cap.* 5. [*To us it sufficeth, that the Bishop of* Rome *is S.* Peter's *Successor, and this all the Fathers testifie, and all the Catholick Church believeth: But whether it be* jure divino *or* humano *is no point of Faith.*]

Ans. 1. Is not that a point of your *Faith* which the General Councils affirm? at least of your Religion? Who can tell then what is your Faith? 2. If an *historical* point be not to be believed from *General Councils*, why should the History of *Peter*'s being at *Rome*, and Bishop there, be believed as from *Fathers*? (which *Nilus* hath said so much against.) 3. Do not the Fathers as much agree that *Peter* was *first Bishop of Antioch*? If then you have no more to shew than they, where is your Title? 4. If your *Divine Right* of succeeding *Peter* be no point of Faith, then he that believeth it not, doth not sin against any point that God would have him believe as from him, and therefore is not to be thought erroneous in the Faith. 5. And yet upon this, which is *no point of Faith*, you build your *Faith* and *Church*, and would have all Christians do the like, on pain of damnation.

II. And

II. And as the *Roman Primacy* was but of *Man's devising*, so I next prove, that it was but *over one Empire*, unless any Neighbours for their own advantage did afterward voluntarily subject themselves. 1. Because the Powers that gave him his Primacy, extended but to the Empire. The Emperour and his Subjects ruled not other Lands.

2. Because the four other Patriarchs, made by the same Power, had no power without the Empire: As appeareth by the distribution of their Provinces in the Council of *Nice*, and afterward: *Pisanus*'s Canons we regard not, that take in *Ethiopia*.

Obj. *The* Abassins *now receive their chief Bishop from the Patriarch of* Alexandria.

That proveth not that ever they were under *Rome*: For there is not the least proof that ever they did so, till *Dioscorus* and his Successors separated from *Rome*, being rejected by them as Hereticks, and by long and flow degrees enlarged their power over many Neighbour Volunteers.

3. Because the *General Councils* in which the Pope presided, were but of the Empire. And the Popes never claimed a more general extensive power then, than the *Councils*: Who indeed with the Emperours made the Papacy in its first state.

4. Because when the Patriarch of *Constantinople* claimed the Primacy, yea called himself *Universal Bishop*, which *Gregory* sharply reprehendeth as Antichristian, yet he never claimed the Government of the whole Christian World, but only of the Empire. And in all their Contests there is no intimation of any such different Claim of the Competitors, as if *Rome* claimed *all the world*, and *Constantinople* but the Empire, or *Roman* World:

World: Their Contest was about the same Churches or Circuit, who should be Chief.

5. The Instances of the several Countries that were never under the Pope, do prove it: Even the great Empire of *Abassia*, and all the rest fore-named without the Empire. Of which and the Exception more under the next.

III. The *General Councils* were all so called only in respect to the generality of the Empire, and not as of all the Christian World; which was never dreamed of. Proved,

1. Because the Emperours that called them (*Constantine, Martian, &c.*) had no power out of the Empire.

2. There is no credible History that mentioneth any further call; much less of all the Christian World.

3. It was the Affairs only of the Empire that the Councils judged of, as is to be seen in all their Canons.

4. The Names of the Bishops yet to be seen, as Subscribers, fully prove it.

5. It was not a thing probable, if possible, that the *Indians*, *Persians*, and other Nations, should send their Bishops into the *Roman* Empire, which was usually at War with them, or dreaded and detested by them.

6. *Theodoret*'s foresaid words of *James* Bishop of *Nisibis* sheweth it [*that he was at the Council of* Nice, *for* Nisibis *was then under the Roman Empire*.]

7. I have oft cited the words of *Reynerius*, saying, that the outer Churches planted by the Apostles were not *under the Church of Rome*.

8. The *executive* part neither could, nor ever was performed upon the Churches without the Empire. When did any Patriarch, or any Provincial, or General Council

cil fend for any Bifhop or other perfon out of *India, Scythia, Ethiopia,* or any other exterior Nation, to anfwer any Accufation? or pafs any Sentence of Depofition, or Sufpenfion againft them? or put any other into their places?

9. General Councils are confeffed by Papifts to be but a *Humane* and not a *Divine Inftitution:* and what Humane Power could fettle them in and over the Church Univerfal? If you fay It is by *Univerfal Confent*; prove to us that ever there *was* fuch a *Confent,* or that ever there was any meeting or treaty for fuch Confent, of all the Chriftian World, and we will yield it to you. Surely if there be any Chriftians at the *Antipodes* they were not fent to in thofe days when *Lactantius, Auguftine,* and others, denyed that there were any *Antipodes,* and derided it; nor when the Pope by our Countryman *Boniface* his Inftigation excommunicated *Virgilius* for holding that there were *Antipodes.* Hear their great difputer *Pighius,* Hierarch. Ecclef. lib. 6. c. 1. fol. 230. [*General Councils* (faith he) *have not a Divine or Supernatural Original, but meerly an Humane Original, and are the Invention of* Conftantine *a Prince; profitable indeed fometimes to find out in Controverfie which is the Orthodox and Catholick Truth, though to this they are not neceffary, feeing it is a readier way to advife with the Apoftolick Seat.*] So that General Councils are *Novel, Humane,* and only of the *Empire* then.

10. But to end all the Controverfie, the names of the Subfcribers are yet to be feen, who were not the reprefentatives of the Chriftian World, but of the *Empire,* as is notorious.

Æneas Sylvius Epift. 288. faith that [*before the Council of Nice there was little refpect had to the Church of Rome.*]

Rome.] And though when he was made Pope, Interest caused him to revoke his judgment of the Councils being above the Pope, he never revoked such historical narratives.

Their great Learned Mathematical (yet militant) Cardinal *Cusanus li. de Concord. Cathol. c.* 13. *&c.* saith [*that the Papacie is but of Positive right, and that Priests are* jure Divino *equal, and that it is subjectional Consent which giveth the Pope and Bishops their Majority, and that the distinction of Dioceses, and that a Bishop be over Presbyters are of Positive Right, and that Christ gave no more to* Peter *than the rest; and that if the congregate Church should chuse the Bishop of* Trent *for their President and Head, he should be more properly* Peter's *Successor than the Bishop of* Rome.]

Object. *Oh but this Book is disallowed by the Pope.*

Answ. No wonder: So is all that is against him.

The Exceptions which we grant are these. 1. There were some Cities of the Empire that were near to other Nations, where the Princes being Heathens, Christians were underlings and few: And the Bishops of these Cities extended their care to as many of the Neighbour Countries as would voluntarily submit to them: So the Bishop of *Tomys* was Bishop of many *Scythians*, and so some that were on the Borders of *Persia*, had many *Persians*, and were at *Nice*.

2. There were some Countries that were sometimes under the *Roman* Power, and sometime under the *Persian*, or others, as Victory carried it; and these when they had been once of the Imperial Church, took it (when they fell under Heathens) to be their Honour, Strength, and Priviledge to be so accounted still, and so would come to their Councils after if they could: So it was

with

with the *Armenians*; and the *Africans*, when the *Gothes* had conquered them, &c.

3. There were some Bishops that lived on the Borders of the Empire, under Heathens, that needed the help of Neighbour Churches, and accordingly were oft with them, craving their help: So it was with the old *Britans*, as to the Bishops of *France*.

4. There were some small Countries adjoining to the Empire, who took the Friendship of the *Roman* Power for their great Honour and safety, and therefore were glad to conform in Religion to the Empire, and to let their Bishops join with them.

5. And there were some Neighbour Countries who were turned to Christianity by the Emissaries of the Bishop of *Rome*; who therefore (rejoicing also in so powerful a Patronage) were willingly his Subjects: But this was long after the first great Councils. These two last were the *Saxons* case in *England*. Accordingly you may sometimes find two or three out of such Countries at some of the General Councils of the Empire. Which yet were called *General* but as to the *Empire*, and not as to the World.

To proceed in the History: When Christians were (mostly) exempted from the Magistrates Judicatures (that were most Heathens, though under a Christian Prince,) and so the *Bishops Canons* were to them, as the *Laws of the Land* are to us, it is no wonder that Councils must then be very frequent, and Canons of great esteem; and hereupon Bishops by prosperity growing more and more worldly and carnal, made use of their Synodical Power, as is aforesaid, to accomplish their own Wills: So that the Synods of Bishops became the great Incendiaries and Troublers of the Empire. You need no more to satisfie you of this, but to read the Acts of the Councils, and the words of *Nazianzen* (called *Theologus*) against Synods and contentious Bishops, and the sad Exclamations of *Hillary Pictav.* They that had too little zeal against Ungodliness, Unrighteousness, Pride, and Malice, were so zealous against any that withdrew from their Power and contradicted them, that they easily stigmatized them for Hereticks, and made even godly sober Christians suspected of Heresie for their sakes; while notorious Vice was used gently in those that adhered unto them. Even holy *Augustine* saith [*Drunkenness is a mortal sin, si sit assidua, if it be daily or constant;* (what, not else?) *and that they must not be roughly and sharply dealt with, but gently and by fair words:*] Vid. Aquin. 22. q. 150. a. 1. 4. ad 4. & a. 2. 1.

And their Great *Gregory,* [*That with leave they must be left to their own wit,* (or disposition,) *lest they grow worse if they be pulled away from such a Custom,*] (as Drunkenness.)

But when it came to such as withdrew from under them, they were not so gentle. *Lucifer Calaritanus* is made the Head of a Heresie, because he was but too much against the receiving of such as had been *Arrians.* The large Catalogues of Heresies contain many that never erred in Fundamentals. They prosecuted the *Priscillianists* so hotly, that if godly men were but given to fasting and strictness of life, they were brought into suspicion of Priscillianism: And the Vulgar took advantage of the Bishops turbulency and ill disposition to abuse the godly. S. *Martin* therefore separated from the whole Synod of the Bishops about him, and neither would join with them, nor have any Communion with them, as supposing them proud men that suppressed piety, and strengthened the wicked,

wicked, by their intemperate profecution: Whereupon they fufpected and accufed him alfo as an unlearned Fellow, and a Favourer of the Prifcillianifts. They did not only bring in the ufe of the Magiftrates Sword in Religion againft Herefie, which *Martin* could not bear, but they owned and flattered an ufurping Emperour, that they might have the help of his Sword to do their work: So that in all thofe parts of *France*, *Germany*, and the Borders of *Italy*, I find not a Bifhop that refufed to own the Ufurper, fave S. *Ambrofe*, and *Martin*, and one *French* Bifhop: And *Sulpitius Severus* tells us that they were men too bad themfelves, and that upon his knowledge *Ithacius* the Leader of them fcarce cared what he faid or did. S. *Cyril* at *Alexandria* is noted by *Socrates* as the firft Bifhop there that ufed the Sword; and his Kinfman S. *Theophilus* went beyond him, and took upon him even to favour the Errour of the *Anthropomorphites*, that he might have their help againft fuch as he hated, and profecuted *Chryfoftom* till he had procured his ejection, which made a rupture in that Church, and caufed the feparation of his Adherents, whom the Bifhop would have taken for a new Sect, and called them *Joannites* ; fuch skill had the domineering fort of Prelates in making and multiplying Herefies and Sects; and calling themfelves ftill the Catholick Bifhops becaufe they kept the upper hand, and major Vote, except where the *Arrians* over-topt them, who then claimed the Catholick Title to themfelves. And by what Arts fome of them kept the favour of the Emperours, to do their work and keep up their greatnefs, *Socrates* tells you in the inftance of the faid S. *Theophilus*, who fent one before the great Battel between *Theodofius* and *Eugenius* another Ufurper, with two Letters, and a rich Prefent, and bid him ftay till the

Battel

Battel was over, and then give the flattering **Letter** and the Present to him whoever that got the better.

But though still since the *world* came into the Church, and the Greatness, Power, and Honour of Prelacy made that Office a very alluring bait to the desires of the most worldly fleshly men, yet God kept up some that maintained their integrity, and bare their testimony against the pride and carnality of the rest; and though the scandals of the Catholicks turned many to the *Novatians*, and other Sects that profest more strictness, (yea *Salvian* makes the *Arrians*, *Gothes*, and *Vandals* themselves to be men of more honesty and temperance than the Catholick Clergie) yet sound Doctrine had still some holy Men that did maintain it.

But what were the *Popes* doing all this while? Sound Doctrine by the advantage of the soundness of the Western Emperour as is said, yet kept out Arrianism, Pelagianisme and such other Heresies there: but they were still striving to be the *Greatest*: *Leo* one of the best of them was one of the first that laid claim to an Universal Headship within the Empire: I told you how *Zosimus* and his Followers strove with the *Africans*, to have Appeals made to *Rome* from the *African* Bishops and Councils: which the *Africans* stifly opposed as contrary to the Canons, to Custom, and to the reason of Discipline, which required that Cases should be judged and ended where persons and things were known, and not by Strangers afar off, where Witnesses could not without intolerable charge and trouble be brought beyond Sea to prosecute the suite. The words of the *African* Council translated are these: [" Let your Holiness, as beseemeth you, repel the " wicked refuges of Presbyters and the Clergie that follow " them, because this is not taken from the *African* Church

by

" by any definitions of the Fathers, and the *Nicene* De-
" crees did most plainly commit both the inferior Clergie
" and the Bishops themselves, to the Metropolitans: for
" they did most prudently and most justly provide that
" all business should be ended in the very places where
" they began, and the Grace of the Holy Ghost will not
" (or should not) be wanting to each province: which
" Equity should by the Priests of Christ be prudently ob-
" served, and most constantly maintained: especially be-
" cause it is granted to every one to appeal to the Coun-
" cils of their own Province, or to an Universal Council,
" if he be offended with the sentence of the Cognitors:
" unless there should be any one that can think that our
" God can (or will) inspire a Justice of tryal into any *One*
" *Man*, and deny it to innumerable Priests that are Con-
" gregated in Council. Or how can that sentence that
" is past beyond Seas be valid, to which the necessary
" persons of the Witnesses could not be brought, because
" of the infirmities of Sexe or Age, many other impedi-
" ments intervening? For that any (that is *Legates*)
" should be sent from the side of your Holiness we find
" not constituted by any Synod of the Fathers (*it seems*
" *they never thought* of a *Divine right*) because that which
" you sent us by our Fellow Bishop *Faustinus* as done by
" the *Nicene* Council --- (*they prove was false*) --- send
" not your Clergy Executors (or *Agitators*) to potent
" men: Do not yield to it, lest we seem to bring the Se-
" cular arrogancy into the Church of Christ, which pre-
" ferreth the light of simplicity and day of humility for
" them that desire to see God: For of our Brother *Fau-*
" *stinus* (*the Popes Legate*) we are secure that the safe
" Brotherly love in your Holinesses honesty and mode-
" ration, can suffer him to stay no longer in *Africa*.]

The

The Popes took this heinously from the *Africans*; that they should stop them in their ascent to the Universal Monarchy: So that Pope *Boniface, Epist. ad Eulal.* saith, [" Aurelius *sometimes Bishop of* Carthage, *with his* " *Colleagues, did begin by the Devils instigation to wax* " *proud against the Church of* Rome, *in the days of our* " *Predecessors* Boniface *and* Celestine.] O how little do proud men instigated by the Devil know themselves, when they think that the Diabolical pride is in them that will not serve their pride!

And *Harding* against *Jewel, Art.* 4. *Sect.* 19. saith [*After the whole* African *Church had persevered in Schism, the space of twenty years, and had removed themselves from the obedience of the Apostolick Seat, being seduced by* Aurelius *Bishop of* Carthage, *&c.*]

Here note, 1. That so numerous were the Bishops in *Africa,* that one of their Provincial Councils had far more Bishops than the Council of *Trent,* or divers others called General. 2. That they were men of the most eminent learning and piety, and that had kept up Discipline above almost any Church in the Empire. S. *Augustine* was one that subscribed the foresaid Letter: and were such Men like to be seduced by *Aurelius*? 3. Note with what Impudencie even such men as *Harding* yet pretend that St *Augustine* was for their Papal Claim, when yet he professeth him to be one of the Schismaticks that cast off obedience to the Seat of *Rome.* 4. Note what good Company we have in our reproach of the same pretended Schism. 5. Note how shamelesly the Papists still tell us of *all the Bishops of the Christian World* being for them, and asking us, *where was our Church before Luther,* that is, a *Society of Christians that obeyed not the Pope*; when they confess that *Augustine* and all the *African* Church for twenty

years

years obeyed him not: (and alas, soon after the *Vandals* came and conquered them, and persecuted and destroyed those famous Bishops that did survive.)

And that you may further know that they had yet more disobedient Resisters than *African* Bishops, you may remember that even the *Egyptian* Monks, so long famous for their great austerity and sanctity, had renounced not only obedience but Communion with the Pope and his Adherents: *Fulgentius* was about going to live with them for their holiness, but he was told of this, and turned his course: *vid. Vit. Fulgent.*

And how great were all those Churches of *Æthiopia*, *Armenia* (*exterior*) *India*, and the rest which the *Apostles converted*, which *Reynerius* aforesaid truly saith, *are not under the Church of* Rome? *Cont. Waldens. Catal. in Biblioth. Patr. To.* 1. *p.* 773.

I have formerly recited the words of *Melch. Canus*, one " of their great Bishops, saying [*Loc. Theolog. li.* 6. *c.* 7. *fol.* " 201. *Not only the* Greeks, *but almost* ALL THE REST " OF THE BISHOPS OF THE WHOLE WORLD " *have vehemently fought to destroy the priviledge of the* " *Church of* Rome. *And indeed they had on their side both* " *the Arms of Emperours, and the* GREATER NUM- " BER OF CHURCHES; *and yet they could never prevail to abrogate the Power of the one Pope of* Rome.

See here their own Confession, 1. Where Christians opposing the Pope were before *Luther*. 2. And of what credit their boast of Universality and Catholick Tradition is. One while (*W. H.*) saith, *The Bishops of the whole World* were for them: But when their cause leads them to tell truth, they say, *Almost all the Bishops of the whole World have vehemently fought against the Pope*, and the Arms of *Emperors and the greater number of Churches were against them.*

P. And

And indeed, if it had been none but the *Greeks*, he might well have said [*The greater number of Churches:*] For the Contest which begun upon the Emperours removal to *Constantinople*, and at the first General Council, increasing more and more, till *Gregory* opposed *John's* Claim of Universal Bishop, as Antichristian, at last *Phocas* the cruel murderer of *Mauritius* gave the Title to the Bishop of *Rome*: But that no whit ended the contest, following Emperors being contrary minded, and the *Greeks* continuing their Claim, the Bishops of *Rome* and *Constantinople* excommunicating one another; so that by this abominable striving which should be the Chief or Greatest, the Churches that were of old in the Empire have been divided, and so they continue to this very Day, as unreconcileable as ever.

And when *Gregory* sent his Emissary hither to Preach to the *Saxons*, they found the Christian *Britans* and *Scots* not only averse to the Government, Orders, and Ceremonies of *Rome* (so that in many Kings Reigns neither words nor force could make them yield) but also such as refused their Communion, and would not so much as eat and drink with them in the same house.

No wonder then that *Marinarius* at the Council of *Trent* complain, *that the Church is shut up in the Corners of* Europe: and that *Sonnius* Bishop of *Antwerp* say (Demonstr. Relig. Christ. li. 2. Tract. 5. c. 3.) [*I pray you what room hath the Catholick Church now in the habitable World?*] *scarce three Elns long in comparison of the vastness which the Satanical Church doth possess.*

The truth is, saith *Brierwood, Divide the known World* (and alas how much is unknown?) *into thirty parts, and about nineteen are Heathens, and six Mahometans, and*

five

five Christians of all sorts: And of these Christians the Papists at this day are as some think about a fifth part, some think a fourth part, and some think a third part.

And after the assuming of the Universal Title, their Popes more and more degenerated to such odious wickedness at last as we hope few Pagans are guilty of: which we speak, not as from Enemies, but from their own Historians and Flatterers, such as *Platina, Baronius, Genebrard, &c.* Nay, not so much from them as from Councils General and Provincial which have accused, condemned, and deposed them. Read in my *Key for Catholicks* pag. 220, 221, 222. the words of *Baronius, Genebrard, Platina: CL. Espensæus, Com. Muss, Guicciardine,* &c. *Nic. Clemangis, Bernard, Alv. Pelagius* say more. Let any impartial man but read the Articles on which the Council at *Constance* condemned and deposed *John* 23: about 70 in number, in which they make him almost as bad as a man out of Hell can be, and indeed say, he was commonly called, [*The Devil incarnate.*]

Read the Articles on which the Council at *Basil* condemned and deposed *Eugenius the Fourth as a perjured wretch, an obstinate Heretick,* and all the rest.

Read the Articles on which another Council deposed *John* 13. *alias* 12. And read the Lives of many more in their own Historians.

And what came the *Church* to when it had such Heads? when *Baronius* saith, *ad an.* 912. that [*the face of the holy Roman Church was exceeding filthy: when the most potent Whores did rule at* Rome, *by whose pleasure Seats were changed, Bishops were given, and which is a thing horrid to be heard, and not to be spoken, their Lovers were thrust into* Peters *Chair, being false Popes, who are not to be written in the Catalogue of the Roman Popes, but only for*

P 2 *the*

the marking of such times: And *what kind of Cardinals, Priests, and Deacons, think you, we must imagine, that these Monsters did chuse, when nothing is so rooted in Nature as for every one to beget his like.*] For *near 150 years,* saith *Genebrard, about fifty Popes were rather Apostatical than Apostolical.*]

And where was their *uninterrupted Succession* all this time?

Pope *Nicolas* in his *Decretals Caranz.* p. 393. 395) saith [*He that by Money or the favour of Men, or Popular or Military Tumults is intruded into the Apostolical Seat, without the Concordant and Canonical Election of the Cardinals and the following religious Clergy, let him not be taken for a Pope nor Apostolical, but Apostatical.*] And of the Clergy he saith [*Priests that commit Fornication cannot have the honour of Priesthood;*] Yea, [*Let no Man hear Mass of a Priest whom he certainly knoweth to have a Concubine or Woman introduced.*] (And shall not *Protestants forgive* those that will not hear such, or as bad?) Where then was the Papacy under such?

For above forty years together there were more Popes than one at once, and sometimes more than two, one dwelling at *Rome,* and another at *Avignion,* or elsewhere: One set up and obeyed by one Party, and another by another Party, each condemning the other as an Usurper. And had the Universal Church then any *one Head*? And with what wickedness are they charged, one destroying what the other was for; see in *Wernerus Fascial.* and my *Key* p. 28, 29, 30.

Wernerus and others say, that *Silvester the second was made Pope by the help of the Devil to whom he did homage, that all might go as he would have it ---- but he quickly met with the End that such have that place their hope in de-*
ceitful

ceitful Devils.] When one Pope cuts another in pieces, and casteth his Carcass into the Water, as unworthy of Christian Burial (as you may find in the Lives of *Formosus* and *Sergius*) must we yet suppose such the Lawful Rulers of the World?

The fourteenth Schisme (faith *wernerus*) *was scandalous and full of confusion, between* Benedict *the Ninth* and five others: *which* Benedict *was wholly vitious, and therefore being damned, appeared in a monstrous and horrid shape, his Head and Tail were like an Asses, the rest of his Body like a Bear, saying, I thus appear because I lived like a Beast. In this Schisme* (faith the Author) *there was no less than six Popes at once.* 1. Benedict *was expulsed.* 2. Silvester *the Third gets in, but is cast out again, and* Benedict *restored.* 3. *But being again cast out,* Gregory *the Sixth is put into his place: Who because he was ignorant of Letters, caused another Pope to be Consecrated with him, to perform Church-Offices, which was the fourth: which displeased many, and therefore a third is chosen instead of the two that were fighting with one another: But* Henry (*the Emperour*) *coming in, deposed them all, and chose* Clement *the Second,* (who was the sixth of them that were alive at once.) In my Opinion this *Gregory* the Sixth shewed himself the honestest Man of them all: Who though he could not read himself had the humility by chusing a Partner to confess his ignorance. And I am perswaded if the question had come before him, which was the truest Translation of the *Hebrew* or *Greek* Text, or such like, the Man would scarce have pretended to *Infallibility* in judging. The *nineteenth Schisme, was between* Innocent *the Second and* Peter Leonis, *and* Innocent (faith the Author) *got the better because he had more on his side.*] A good Title no doubt! and thence a good Succession.

The

The twentieth Schisme (saith *wernerus*) was great between Alexander *the Third and four others, and it lasted seventeen years.*

After Nicolas *the Fourth* (saith he) *there was no Pope for two years and a half* (where was the Church then?) and Celestine *the Fifth that succeeded him resigning it,* Boniface *the Eighth entered, that stiled himself Lord of the whole World in Spirituals and Temporals; of whom it was said, he entered as a Fox, lived as a Lyon, and dyed like a Dog.* I have as good hope of the salvation of Celestine the Fifth and *Felix* the Fifth as any two of them, because as they were drawn in as simple Men in ignorance, so their resignation shewed some hope that they repented.

The 22. *Schisme* (saith *wernerus ad an.* 1373.) *was the worst and most subtil Schisme of all that were before it: for it was so perplexed that the most Learned and Conscientious Men were not able to find out to whom they should adhere: And it was continued for forty years to the great scandal of the whole Clergie, and the great loss of souls, because of Heresies and other evils that then sprung up, because there was no discipline in the Church against them. And therefore from this* Urban *the* Sixth *to the time of* Martin *the Fifth, I know not who was Pope.*] (Nor I neither: nor any one else I think).

The twenty third Schisme, was between *Felix* the Fifth and *Eugenius* the Fourth, of which saith *wernerus* [*Hence arose great contention among the Writers of this Matter,* pro & contra, *and they cannot agree to this day:* For one part saith *that a Council is above the Pope*; the other part on the contrary saith, *no, but the Pope is above the Council: God grant his Church Peace, &c.*] The Christian World being all in Divisions because of sidings for these several Popes, the Emperours were constrained to call

call General Councils to end the Schifmes: That at *Conſtance* thought they had done the Work; but they left Work enough for that at *Baſil*, and more than they could do: When they found not a fit Man among the Clergy, they choſe a Lay-man to be Pope, the Duke of *Savoy*, a Man noted for honeſt Simplicity and Piety, and called him *Felix* the Fifth: But *Eugenius*, who was caſt out by the Council for his wickedneſs, kept the place, and made the Duke glad to reſign and leave the Popedome.

Should I ſtay to tell you after the Barbarous Age 900. what work the Popes made in the World, how many thouſand they forced to death upon the Wars at *Jeruſalem*; how many ſcore thouſand *waldenſes* and *Albigenſes* they Murdered; How they forced Kings to kiſs their Feet, and trod on the Neck of *Frederick* the Emperour: How they divided the Empire by a Rebellious War againſt the Emperours *Henry* the Third and Fourth; And how they Armed their Subjects and Neighbours againſt them, yea the Emperours Son againſt his own Father; And how the Writers of thoſe times are divided, and open the lamentable Diviſions of the Ages in which they lived; What work they made here againſt the Kings of *England*; and what paſſed between *Boniface* the Eighth and the King of *France*, and the Coin on which he Stamped his Reſolution to *deſtroy* Babylon, &c. you would little think that either *Holineſs* or *Unity* were any Property of the *Roman* Church.

Qu. *But if moſt did not favour them, how did they aſcend to ſo great power?* Anſ. 1. The old Name of the *Imperial Rome*, and the *Popes Primacie* in the *Empire*, kept up a Veneration for him in the ignorant. 2. The Eaſtern Emperours ſeated at *Conſtantinople* were ſo taken up with Wars, Rebellions, and other Difficulties

at

at home, that they could not take sufficient care of the West; but left the Popes too much advantage to grow great: and wickedness also increasing among them (though the Princes presence kept *their Patriarchs* in more order and submission, than the Popes that were become masterless) provoked God to give them up to be conquered by the *Mahometan Turks*: And by the Ambition of the Popes, the Emperours wanted the due assistance of their Western Subjects, to resist their Enemies. And the Pope took the advantage of the Eastern Emperours weakness, to lead the West into a settled Rebellion, offering the King of *France* the Western Empire, which he embraced, the Pope making his Bargain with him for his own advantage. 3. And in the Wars of Christian Princes, the Pope used to obtrude his Arbitration, in such a manner as tended to his gain: so that he shortly got to be a temporal Prince of a great part of *Italy*, and to have Crowns and Kingdoms made feudatary to him. 4. And he got *Germany* to be broken into so many small Republicks and Liberties, as that they were not able to unite to resist him. 5. And he took great advantage of the religious humours of any that were devout, and allowed them so many and various Societies, and with so great Priviledges, as obliged them generally to uphold and serve him: Though he cruelly persecuted all that were against his Power and Interest, yet he allowed almost all the Diversities of such as would but unite in him and serve him. 6. And as he so twisted his own and all his Clergies Interest, that they were all ready to obey and defend him against their several Princes, and thereby had a great power in every Christian State in *Europe*, so, keeping all his Clergie unmarryed, their wealth still accumulated and flowed into the Church: And the Eastern Empire being

first

firſt weakned and then overthrown, and the Weſtern Nations kept weak, and in continual Wars againſt each other, there was none well able to refiſt his Pride, but one party ſtill was ready to flatter him, partly to keep their own Clergy in Peace, and partly to have his help againſt their Enemies.

And the grand Cheat by which they were commonly deceived was, that they lookt more at his preſent poſſeſſion of Primacie, than at the reaſon and right by which he claimed it; and ſo he that had been Prime Patriarch in one Empire, ſet up by the Prince, ſtill claimed the right of the ſame places when the Empire was diſſolved: as if the Subjects of the Kings of *France*, *Spain*, &c. muſt obey him, becauſe they did ſo when they were the Subjects of *Conſtantine*, *Theodoſius*, *Valentinian*. &c. For by little and little he changed his Title mentioned in the Council of *Calcedon*, into a pretended *Divine Right*, and ſo they that would not have obeyed him as ſet up by *Cæſar* and his Councils, obeyed him as if he had been ſet up by God: For the name of St. *Peter and his Chair and Succeſſour* was uſed as the common blind.

And next to that he did by degrees change his claim of a *Primacie in the Empire* into a claim of Primacie in *all the World*: and his claim of a meer *Primacie*, into a claim of *Soveraignty*, or *Governing Monarchy*.

If you ask me, how could he blind Men ſo far as to make ſuch a change? You ſeem not to know Man-kind, nor to obſerve common experience. Do you not conſider what power the Clergie had every where got with the People? What an advantage poſſeſſion and St. *Peters* name were? And how lamentably ignorant they kept the People? Do we not ſee that even in our more knowing times, yea among Proteſtants, yea with ſome

Q   Divines,

Divines, the evident distinction between their *Humane Right* and their pretended *Divine Right*, and between an *Universal Council or Church of the Empire*, and of the *whole World*, have not been sufficiently observed in our Disputes against them?

And the additional Countries of voluntary Subjects in *Brittain*, *Hungary*, *Sweden*, *Denmark*, &c. which of later times, since his Imperial *Primicie*, have fallen in to him, have much helped to blind the people herein, and to serve his Claim as by Divine Right. For which ends his Emissaries have taken great pains, at the East and West *Indies*, in *China*, and *Japan* and *Congo*, (and once they made an attempt in *Abassia*,) and among the *Greeks* and in many other Nations of the World; laudably seeking to win some Heathens to Christ, that they might win them to the Pope; and turbulently seeking to disturb the *Greeks* and other Christian Churches, to draw them to the obedience of the Pope.

The Doctrines by which they promote their design are more than I may now stay to open.

I. One of the chief is, by depressing the Honour of the sacred Scriptures, as insufficient to acquaint us with all Gods will that is necessary to our salvation, without *supplemental Tradition*; that so all men might be brought to depend on them as the Keepers of Tradition.

But 1. Is their Tradition yet written in any of their own *Books*, or not? If not, where are they kept? And who knoweth what they are? Is it not strange that so many Doctors in so many Ages, all remembring them, would none of them ever write them down? Are they in the Memory of the Pope only? (What of those that could not read, or that were condemned as Hereticks or Infidels?) Then all the World must receive them from

the

the Popes Memory. If so, must it be *word or writing*? And had he no Memory of them before he was Pope? But if it be in *other Mens* Memories that your unwritten Traditions are kept, in whose is it? If in all the Doctors of your Church, why did not *Luther, Melancthon, Pet. Martyr* and the rest that turned from you, know them? Or did they suddenly *forget* them all when they turned Protestants? And how vast must your necessary Religion be, if yet it must have more in it unwritten, than is to be found in all your great Volumes of Councils, and your huge Library?

But I suppose you will say that all your unwritten Traditions are *now written*: If so, they are not *unwritten*: And *how long* have they been written, and by whom? If Fathers and Sons could keep them unwritten in memory a thousand years, why not 1100, and why not 1600? *&c.* If they were written in the beginning, where be the Books? Are they not such as other Christians can read and understand as well as you, (or an illiterate Pope?) If there be a necessity of having them in writing now, was there not the same necessity to former Ages?

2. I suppose you will send us to your *Councils* for those *Traditions*: But if the Bishops know them not before they come to the Council, how do they begin to know them then? Do they go thither for a new miraculous Revelation of an old Tradition left with the whole Church?

1. But do not Councils oft determine things confessedly uncertain to the Church before; and yet out of utter uncertainty, it suddenly becometh an Article of Faith? For Instance, the great Council at *Basil* saith (*Bin. sess.* 36. *p.* 80.) [" A hard Question hath been in divers parts

" and

"and before this Synod, about the Conception of the
"glorious Virgin *Mary*, and the beginning of her Sancti-
"fication: Some saying that the Virgin and her Soul was
"for some time, or instant of time, actually under Origi-
"nal Sin: Others on the contrary saying, that from the
"beginning of her Creation God loving her gave her
"Grace, by which preserving and freeing that blessed
"Person from the Original Spot----We having diligently
"lookt into the Authorities and Reasons which for many
"years past have in publick relation on both sides been
"alledged, before this holy Synod, and having seen ma-
"ny other things about it, and weighed them by ma-
"ture consideration, do *Define* and *Declare*, That the Do-
"ctrine affirming That the glorious Virgin *Mary* the Mo-
"ther of God, by the singular preventing and opera-
"ting Grace of God, was never actually under Original
"Sin, but was ever free from all Original and actual Sin,
"and was holy and immaculate, is to be approved, held
"and embraced of all Catholicks as godly and conso-
"nant to Church-worship, Catholick Faith, right Rea-
"son, and sacred Scripture: and that henceforth it shall
"be lawful for no Man to Preach or Teach the con-
"trary.

Where was this Tradition kept before, that was so hard a Controversie till now?

2. And do not General Councils bring in Novelties? I cited formerly the words of *Cajetan* in his Oration in the Council at the *Laterane* under *Leo* 10. charging the Council of *Constance*, *Basil* and *Pisa* with Novelty, and such Novelty as would have quite defaced the Church and was inconsistent with it. And *Pighius* charg- eth them with the like. Yea I told you before where he saith that General Councils themselves are a Novelty de- vised by *Constantine*.

3. Be

3. Be not General Councils themselves approved or reprobated at the pleasure of the Pope? What a number of reprobated Councils were there? that yet were as numerous as the approved, and as lawfuly called and assembled. *Bellarmine* instanceth in the 2. of *Ephesus*, *Constance*, *Basil*, and many more: Of which more before.

II. Another of their deceits is by pretending to *Vinc. Lerinensis* Rule, *quod ab omnibus, ubique, semper,* &c. as if *Antiquity* and *Universality* were on their side. I must remember that I have long ago confuted these and the rest of their deceits in my *Key for Catholicks*: Yet I will briefly speak here to these two.

1. For *Antiquity* we willingly stand to it, and to the rejecting of all Novelty in Religion: But we must have better proof than the word of our Grand-fathers, or a Priest. 1. Is any of their Books or Traditions elder than the holy Scripture? 2. Either the *Greeks, Armenians, Abassines, &c.* have been sure Keepers of *Antiquity*, or not: If yea, then we may take their Testimony as well as the Church of *Romes*. If not, why may not you prove as ill Keepers of it as they?

3. But are they not *certain Novelties* that you would impose on us under the colour of *Antiquity*? Read but *Pet. Moulin de Novit. Papismi*, or Mr. *Th. Doelittles* Discourse in the *Morning Lectures* against Popery, and you shall see the Novelty of your Religion fully proved. Take now but these few instances. 1. Your very *Patriarchate*, *Primacie*, Claim of Universality, General Councils, are all proved Novelties before.

2. Your own Writers confess that the denying the People *Christi Blood* (or the Cup) in the Lords Supper is, a Novelty, that prevailed by Custom by little and little;

and

and was not common long before the Council at *Constance*: Dare you say that it was so from the beginning, or of old?

3. Can you possibly believe that your forbidding men to read the Scriptures in a known Tongue without a Licence is not a Novelty, if ever you read *Chrysostom, Augustine, Jerome*, or any thing of the Ancients?

4. Is it not a Novelty for the publick Prayers of the Church to be ordinarily made in a Tongue not understood by the generality of the People? But I must stop.

2. And as to *Universality* I have before proved, 1. That by their own Confession most of the Churches and Bishops of the World have been against them. 2. That at this day they are not above the third part of Christians. Too small an Universal Church for any man of Charity and Consideration to be a member of: A Sect that call themselves *All the Church*. *Jacob. a Vitr. Histor. Orient. Cap.* 77. tells us that, *the Churches in the Easterly part of* Asia *alone exceeded in multitude both the Greek and Latine Churches.*

As for their telling us that all these followed *Dioscorus* a Heretick, or were *Nestorians*, and that all the *Abassines, Armenians, Georgians, Syrians, Coptics, Greeks, Protestants, &c.* are Hereticks, or Schismaticks, I have answered it so oft at large that I must not repeat what I have said. Only, 1. I say that if the Censures and Revilings of Adversaries can un-christen all others, and appropriate the Church to them that have least Charity, perhaps the Quakers may shortly have as fair a Title as the Papists. If *General Councils* be not to be believed when they Hereticate Popes, I will not believe a Railer when he Hereticates most of the Christian World, whom he never saw or spake with. Surely that man judgeth persons unheard.

unheard. 2. I repeat the words of *Burchardus* one of your own, that long lived among them, and spake what he saw, p. 325, 326. [*And as for those that we judge to be damned Hereticks, as the* Nestorians, Jacobites, Maronites, Georgians, *and the like, I found them to be for the most part good and simple men, and living sincerely towards God and Men, they are of great abstinence, &c.* ------ And p. 324. he saith, that [*the* Syrians, Greeks, Armenians, Georgians, Nestorians, Nubians, Jubeans, Chaldeans, Maronites, Ethiopians, Egyptians, *and many other Nations of Christians there inhabit; and that some are Schismaticks not subject to the Pope, and others called Hereticks, as the* Nestorians, Jacobites, *&c. but there are many in these Sects that are very simple, knowing nothing of Heresies; devoted to Christ, macerating the Flesh with Fastings, and clothed with the most simple Garments, so that they far excel the very* RELIGIOUS *of the Church of* Rome.] And, p. 323. of the Papists, whom he calleth by the Name of Christians, as if it were proper to them, he saith, [*There are in the Land of Promise men of every Nation under Heaven, and every Nation liveth after their own Rites; and to speak the very truth to our own great confusion, there are none found in it that are worse and more corrupt in Manners than Christians,*] (that is, Papists.)

3. If greater Errours and Vices than are among the *Armenians,* the *Abassines, Syrians, &c.* will allow us to reject men from our Communion, how much more cause have we to renounce Communion with Popes and Papists than with these Churches?

4. How can any man say that Nations and Countries are to be rejected as Hereticks, unless the single persons guilty were tryed and heard? when there is no Heresie

but

but what is in individuals, and no Law of God or Reason condemneth the innocent for the guilties faults; much less all Posterity for their Ancestors.

III. But they never gain more than by aggravating the Divisions that are among other Christians, and boasting of the Unity of their Church: And the Contentions that have been among us have given them such advantage, as that some in the sense of their former guilt, having been Sect-masters themselves, have turned Papists, as thinking it the state of Union; and having found no settlement in those ways which they have tryed, because they never rightly understood the true temperament of the Christian Religion which they professed, they think to find it in that way that they never tryed; as sick men turn from side to side for ease, while the cause of their weariness and pain is within them, and turneth with them.

Here let the Reader note, 1. That Fools judge of Differences in Religion by the *noise* that it makes in the World; but men of Reason judge of it by the *greatness* and *number* of the points of Difference. Verily our Differences here in *England*, and the Neighbour Protestant Churches, have shewed in us much personal peevishness, unskilfulness, and other faults; but in my judgment they are such as greatly commend our *real concord* in the same Religion, and partly our *Conscience* in valuing it, and being loth to lose it.

If you see Latine Grammarians reviling one another, about the *spelling* or *pronunciation* of a word or two, and critically contending with *Varro*, *Gellius*, &c. which is the right, when a man that never knew a word of Latine but Welch or Irish, never strove about such Questions in his life; which of these will you think have more
agreement

agreement in their Language? I would say that those men that disagree but about the pronunciation of a few words are very much agreed, in comparison of a Barbarian, that agreeth not with them in a Sentence or a Word. Even the old Schoolmen were in Language more agreed with *Erasmus*, *Faber*, *Hutten*, and other Critical Grammarians that derided them, than any illiterate man was with any of them. All *Gruterus* his Volumes of Grammatical Controversies, shew not so much distance in Language, as the peaceable silence of an unlearned man doth.

And no one strives much about that which he doth not much care for: Countrymen can contemptuously laugh at Logical Disputes or Criticisms. Horses or Oxen will not strive with us for our Gold or Jewels, Clothes or Food, as we do with one another; and yet they are not so like us in the *estimation* of such things, as we are to one another.

When I hear religious persons contentiously censuring each other, about some little points of Ceremony, Order, Discipline, or Form, which are but the *fimbria*, or the Welts and Laces of Religion, I am angry at their weakness and defect of love; but I must needs think that there is very great concord in the *Faith* and *Religion* (Objective) of these men, who differ about no greater matters than such as these. If men that were building a Palace would fall together by the Ears, only about the driving of a Pin, I should marvel at their concord that differed in no more; though I could wish them, like wrangling Children, whipt for their folly and frowardness till they were quiet. The *great* things that *Protestants* have paltrily wrangled about, are, 1. The Doctrinal Controversies called *Arminian*: 2. And the matters of *Discipline*. and *Ceremonies*. The former I have shewed lately in a large Volume, hath much more of *verbal* than of *real difference*, and is cherished by the ambiguity of words, aud the unskilfulness of too many to discuss those ambiguities, and find out exactly the true state of the Controversie: It is oft but Stubble that maketh the greatest blaze.

And as for the other, I would not undervalue the least things of Religion, but I will say, that *Engagement*, *Faction* and *worldly Interest* are magnifying Glasses to many men, and make a Mote to seem a Beam, and a Gnat to seem a Camel. And it is one of the Devils old Wiles, to keep men from learning of Christ, how to Worship the Father of Spirits, in spirit and truth, by starting such Questions, as, *whether in this Mountain or at Jerusalem men ought to worship?* and to hinder *godly edifying by doting about questions that gender strife*. And fighting for Shoo-buckles may shew the quarrelsomness of men, but it proveth not the Greatness of the matter.

2. Note further that though *Subjective Religion* (the *measures* of our belief, Love and Obedience) be as various as persons are; yet the *Objective Religion of all true Protestants* is the same: Not only the same in the Essentials (*one God, one Saviour and Lord, one Baptismal Covenant, one Creed, one Spirit, one Body of Christ, and one Hope of Glory,* Eph. 4. 4, 5, 6.) but also the same in all the *Integral parts*: For it is *Integrally* the *Holy Scripture* which containeth all that they take (with the Law of Nature) to be the whole Law of God, and so the Rule of Divine *Faith, Desire* and *Duty*. They may *subjectively* have some difference in understanding some Texts, (as the most Learned and holy in the world have:)
But

But *Objectively* they have no other Divine Faith or Religion.

3. And note, that the Church that *Protestants*, yea *Greeks, Armenians, Syrians, Abassines* are of, are all certainly one and the same Church: For a Church is constituted of the *Ruling* and the *Ruled* Parts. And they perfectly agree that *Christ* is the only Essentiating and Universal Head; In him they all unite, and confess that there is no other. Even the Patriarch of *Constantinople*, as I have shewed, claimeth but a Primacie in the Empire, and not the Government of all the World, no not of us in *England*.

And as for the Ruled Constitutive part, we are agreed that it is All *Baptized Christians* that have not apostatized, nor forsaken any Essential part of Christianity, nor are excommunicate by Power from Christ. So that we are clearly all of one and the same Church.

But how far the Papists differ in the *Greatness* and *number* of their Controversies, I think to tell you a little more anon.

IV. I may not stay to shew at large, how they vary their shape and course as may fit their Interest: How sometime they put on the person of Infidels or Atheists to plead men into an uncertainty of all Religion, that they may be loose enough to follow them into theirs: For even so *Car. Boverius* would have perswaded our late King, *Apparat. ad Consult.* [*The first thing is* (saith he) *seeing true Religion is to be inquired after by you, that before you address your self to search for it, you first have all Religions in suspicion with you; and that you will so long suspend* (or take off) *your mind and will from the Faith and Religion of the Protestants, as you are in searching after the truth.*]

R 2 Reader,

Reader, doth not this tell you whence much of our late Atheism and Infidelity cometh, and what it tendeth to? I tell thee not the words of a Novice, but a person chosen to have seduced our King, when he was Prince, in *Spain*. And is not this way very suitable to the end? How must men become Papists? *Boverius* will teach you: First " *suspect* all Religion, and with your very *Mind* and *will* " cease to believe that there is a God, or that he is Pow- " erfull, Wise or Good, or that we are his Creatures and " Subjects, or that there is any Heaven or Hell or Life to " come, or that Christ is not a Deceiver but a Saviour, " or that any of the Bible is true: Cease from Loving, " Fearing, Obeying or trusting God, and from loving " man for his sake: Cease praying to him, and forbear- " ing any wickedness, injustice, cruelty, perjury or fil- " thiness as being forbidden by him, and this as long as " you are searching after the truth.] Verily this devil- ish counsel is so notoriously followed now by some, that we may fear what truth it is that they are searching after. Certainly this way is of the Devil, and how it can lead to God I know not. I love *Cartesian* Philosophy the worse because its principle is so congruous to this.

And their Doctrine of lawful hiding their Religion by Equivocation is commonly known. And what they say about coming to our Churches I have formerly cited at large out of *Thom. a Jesu*, and the lawfulness of denying the person of a Clergie-man or a Religious man: And the ground of all, [*because humane Laws for the most part bind not the Subjects Conscience when there is great hazard of life, as Azorius* hath well taught, *Inst. Moral.* To. 1. l. 8. c. 27. See the Authors words *de Convers. Gent.* li. 5. Dub. 4. pag. 218. and Dub. 5. p. 218, 219. and Dub. 6. p. 220.

We may find them in our Churches and garb when their intereſt requires it. But again I muſt for all theſe points refer the Reader to *my forementioned Book* (*A Key for Catholicks.*)

The hiſtory of the Papacie being thus briefly given you, I ſhould next briefly tell you, I. What a Pope is; II. What a Papiſt is; III. What the preſent Papal Church is: But it requireth more than this ſhort Writing, to open any one of theſe to the full: But take this breviate.

CHAP. VI.

What the Pope is.

I. WE are not to deſcribe the Biſhop of *Rome* as he was at the beginning, but as in that Stature to which he is ſince grown up. And ſo unmeaſurable a Potentate muſt be deſcribed to you but *by parts, and inadequate Conceptions*; And I will no more undertake to enumerate all, than to Name all the Kingdoms known and unknown to us *Europeans* which he claimeth the Government of. But I remember who it was that ſhewed Chriſt all the Kingdoms of the world, and ſaid, *All theſe things will I give thee if thou wilt fall down and worſhip me, Math. 4. 9.* Or as *Luk. 4. 6. All this Power will I give thee and the Glory of them, for that is delivered to me, and to whomſoever I will I give it.*

I. *The Pope of* Rome *is an Uſurper, who from the lawful Epiſcopacy of one particular Church aſpired to be a Biſhop over many Churches and Biſhops, and a Metropolitan, and thence to be a Patriarch,* and the *firſt Patriarch in the* Roman *Empire in order of Dignity, and entred a Contest for the Primacie with his Competitor of* Constantinople, *which is not ended to this day; And next claimed an Universal Government in the Empire as well as a Primacy; And also the Government of such Neighbour Churches as had once been in the Empire, or had been lately converted by any of his Clergie; And lastly being made a King of* Rome *or Secular Prince in* Italy, *he also claimed a Monarchy or Government over all the world under the name of Ecclesiastical.*]

All this is proved in the foregoing History of the Papacy, and may better be found out by any that will peruse the History of the Church and Empire, than by particular Citations.

II. *By the name of Ecclesiastical power he understandeth not only that which is truly spiritual or sacerdotal, by which Gods word is preached and applyed to particular persons, by reception into Christian Communion, and exclusion from it, sententially; But also a power of erecting Courts of Judicature in all Kingdoms to judge of cases about Ministers, Temples, Tythes, Testaments, Administration of Goods, Lawfulness of Marriages, Divorces and many such like, in a manner of Constraint which is proper to the Magistrate:* Abusively calling *this the Ecclesiastical Power* in foro exteriore, *distinct from the sacerdotal* in foro interiore, *cheating the world with words.*

Experience fully proveth this.

III. *For the performance of this Deceit they appropriate to Princes and other Magistrates the Titles of* [CIVIL] *or* [SECULAR] *making the world believe that as Soul and Body differ, so the Pope and his Clergie being Governours of the Soul, or in order to salvation, excel Kings and Magistrates who are but Governours for bodily welfare and Civil Peace.*

Whereas

Whereas indeed the difference of the Offices of *Christian Magistrates* and *Pastors*, is not, that one is but for the *Body* and the other for the *Soul*; for both are to further mens Salvation, and true Religion, and the obedience of Gods Laws in order thereto: But it is in this, that Princes and Magistrates have the Power of Governing men in things Secular and Religious within their true Cognisance *by the Sword*, that is, by *external Compulsion and Coercion*, by *Mulcts and Penalties* forcibly executed; whereas the Pastors have only the Charge of Teaching men *Christs Doctrine*, and Guiding the Church in the administration of Gods Worship, and by the *Keys or Authority* from Christ, judging who is capable or uncapable of Church Communion, and declaring pardon and Salvation to the penitent for their Comfort, and the contrary to the impenitent for their humiliation; and all this only *by word of Mouth, without any Constraining force*.

Proof of the Character.

Pope *Innoc.* 3. (*vid. &* Cosins *Hist. Transub.* p. 147, 148) [" *God made two great Lights in the Firmament of Heaven,—and of the Universal Church*; that is, he instituted two Dignities, which are the Pontifical Authority and the Regal Power: But that which ruleth the Day, that is, things spiritual, is the greatest, and that which ruleth carnal things is the less: that it may be known that the difference between Popes and Kings is such as is the difference between the Sun and the Moon.

If this were true, the lowest Priest were incomparably more honourable or amiable than Kings, as the Soul is more excellent than the Body: But *David, Solomon, Hezekiah, Josiah*, and all good Kings, did shew that

that Religion was the matter of their Government and the principal part of their care. Read for this fully Bishop *Bilson* of Christian obedience, Bishop *Buckeridge* for the Magistrates Power, and Bishop *Andrews Tortura Torti*; excellent discourses against the Papal Usurpation.

IV. *The Office which he thus claimeth as over all the Earth, is to be the Vicar of Christ or of God, or the Vice-Christ or Vice-God, as Kings have their Vice-Kings in remote Provinces.*

Proved.

I have elsewhere cited the words of Popes saying, that they are *Vice-Christi* and *Vice-Dei*, at large: And Pope *Julius*'s words [*we holding the place of the Great God, the Maker of all things and all Laws:*] And Carol. Boverius's words, *Consult. de. Rat. fidei*, &c. to our late King, saying [*Besides Christ the Invisible Head of the Church, there is a necessity, that we acknowledge another certain visible Head, subrogate to Christ and instituted of him*, &c.] And *Card. Betrand's* words in *Biblioth. Patrum*, that saith, *Almighty God had not been wise else, if he had not sent One only to Govern the world under him:*] And *Boverius* reason [*Christ was himself on Earth once a visible Monarch; And if the Church had need of a visible Monarch, it hath need of one still.*] Christ said that it was necessary that he went away that the Paraclete might come, whom *Tertullian* calleth his *Agent*; But the Papists will not part with him so, but they will have his *Body* here still, and yet a Vice-Christ or visible Monarch also in his stead: See their own words, which I have cited at large in my Answer to Mr. *Johnson*.

V. *The pretended ground of this his Claim is, that St.*
Peter

Peter received this power from Christ, and that St. Peter *was Bishop last at* Rome, *and that the Pope succeedeth him in his Bishoprick, and Power.*

This is professed commonly by them.

But 1. It is false that St. *Peter* received any such Power from Christ, as to be the Governour of all the rest of the Apostles and Christians in the World: He never exercised or claimed such a Government, but in cases of Controversie *Act.* 15. and *Gal.* 2, &c. He dealeth but on equal terms with the rest. And they that said *I am of Cephas,* are as well rebuked as they that said, *I am of Paul.*] And 1 *Cor.* 12. 28, 29, &c. Apostles are said to be but *chief Members* of the Church, and *Christ* the only *Head*: And when the Disciples strove who should be the greatest, Christ giveth it not to *Peter*, but forbideth it to them all: And *Peter* himself as a fellow Elder exhorteth all Elders to oversee and feed the Flock, *not as Lords over the Heritage,* &c. and never claimeth a Soveraignty to himself. No word mentioneth any Power that St. *Peter* had greater than his Apostleship: And *Bellarmine* professeth that the Pope hath not his power as succeeding him in his Apostleship, but as an ordinary Pastor over the whole Church.

2. There is no certainty that ever *Peter* was at *Rome* (as *Nilus* hath shewed;) but a humane Testimony of many later Fathers, upon the words of uncertain Reporters before them, which are to be believed indeed as probable but no more; There being as great a number of Papist Writers I think (about 60) that tell us there was a Pope *Joane,* and yet it is uncertain if not least probable. But if he was at *Rome,* Apostles were no where proper Bishops. Bishops were the fixed Elders or Pastors of particular Churches: Apostles were moveable and Itinerant,

rant, having an Indefinite Commission to go preach the Gospel to all the world as far as they were able. Though the ancient Fathers used to call them Bishops because *pro tempore* they Ruled (perswasively) where they came: Though indeed their work was to settle Churches and Bishops, and not to be settled Bishops themselves.

3. *Paul* was certainly and long at *Rome*, and liker to be as a Bishop there of the two: If *Paul* was not one, *Peter* was not; for there is no more, but less proof of his Government there. If *Paul* was one, then one City had two, contrary to the old Canons.

4. There is no proof that *Peter's* being *last at Rome* gave his Power to all or any following Bishops of *Rome*, any more than to the Bishops of *Antioch* who are said to succeed him in his first Bishoprick; or any more than Chrifts dying at *Jerusalem*, the Mother Church, did fix the Supremacie there: or any more than the other eleven Apostles did leave their power which they had above all ordinary Bishops, to the places where they abode (either last or first.) If *Peter's* dying Bishop at *Rome* prove such a succession of Universal Monarchy, the aforesaid Successions will be proved by the same Reason; which yet none affirm: Even *Alexandria* claimed but from St. *Mark* who was less than thirteen Apostles: But no *Testament* of *Peter* declaring any conveyance of such a Monarchy is pretended by the Popes (which is a wonder:) Nor any word that ever he used of such importance.

5. I have shewed that General Councils (*Calced.* and *Constant.*) have declared that *Romes* primacy had a later humane rise.

Yet would they have exercised no other Government than St. *Peter* did, the world would not have been troubled by them as they have been.

VI. *The*

VI. *The Papists seem not resolved themselves whether the Pope have an Universal Apostleship or Teaching office, as well as the Universal Monarchy or Government.*

Though *Bellarmine* say that he succeedeth not *Peter* as an *Apostle*, but as a *Pastor*; yet most others that I have seen medling with it, say otherwise. If he succeed not in the Apostleship, he is no true Successour of St. *Peter* at all, in any supereminence of Power: For what he had was as an Apostle: If he do, then he is bound to go preach himself to the Nations of the world as *Peter* was: To send others to preach, and not do it himself was no *Apostleship*: They were sent themselves. *David* and *Solomon* set up Priests, and yet were themselves no Priests: *Hezekiah* and *Josiah* sent and set up Preachers, and yet undertook not that office themselves.

VII. *This Pope claimeth the sole Power of calling General Councils of all the Christian world (yet never did it) And consequently of being the Judge when any shall be called, and so whether ever there shall be any or not. And though former General Councils voted that they should be every ten years, yet he prevaileth to the contrary.*

VIII. *Also he claimeth the sole power of presiding in such Councils, and also of making their Decrees either valid by his approbation or null or invalid by his Reprobation, as he please: so that nothing that they Decree is of force but as it pleaseth him; whence we have distinct Catalogues of Approved and Reprobate Councils.*

Yet no mortal man knoweth oftentimes how much of a Councils Acts and Decrees the Pope approveth. When *Martin* the fifth had consented to all done by the Council of *Constance*, the word [*Conciliariter acta*] seemed to the Council to mean [*all that they did de facto as a Council.*]

Council.] But the Popes ever since yet reject that Council on pretense that by [*conciliariter*] was meant *all that de jure as a Council they might do.* *Gregory* the first approved of the four first General Councils, receiving them as the four Gospels (and if his Predecessors did not, it was because their consent was not taken to be necessary, nor much sought.) And yet now *Bellarmine* raileth at the Council of *Calcedon*, and they tell us how much of it they receive and how much not. And so of many others.

And nothing is more evident in such History, than that the Emperors and not the Pope, were they that called divers of the first Councils.

IX. *The Pope accordingly claimeth a supremacy above General Councils; that he may dissolve them, but they cannot question or depose him; though General Councils have decreed the contrary.*

I recited *Binnius* words before, *Vol.* 2. *p.* 515. *Pighius*, *Gretser's*, *Bellarmine's*, and multitudes more might soon be produced to the same sense; The eighth General Council at *Constantinople* saith, *Can.* 21. that [" None " must compose any Accusations against the Pope] Vid. " *Bellarm. de concil. li.* 2. c. 11.

Saith *Pighius*, Hier. Eccl. li. 6. [" The Councils of *Con-*
" *stance* and *Basil* went about by a new trick and pernicious
" example to destroy the Ecclesiastical Hierarchy, and in-
" stead of it to bring in the domination of a promiscuous
" confused popular multitude; that is, to raise again *Ba-*
" *bylon* it self; subjecting to themselves, or the Commu-
" nity of the Church (which they falsly pretended that they
" represented) the very Head and Prince of the whole
" Church: and him that is the Vicar of Christ himself in
" this his Kingdom; and this against Order and Nature,
"against

"against the clearest light of Gospel Verity, against all
"Authority of Antiquity, and against the undoubted faith
"and judgment of the Orthodox Church it self.] (And
yet our Papists would perswade us that their Grandfathers,
much less great General Councils cannot bring in Novelties on pretense of Antiquity, and mislead them.) Truly
said *Lud. Vives, in August. de Civ. Dei* l. 20. c. 26 [" Those
"are taken by them for Edicts and Councils which make
"for them; the rest they no more regard than a meet-
"ing of Women in a Work-house or a Washing-
place.]

X. *He claimeth a power of Legislation to all the Christian World, Kings, and States, and single Subjects; and
that no Kings can nullifie his Laws to their own Subjects:
As also the power of receiving Accusations and Appeals,
and of judging and executing accordingly.*

This needeth no proof, being not denyed.

XI. *He claimeth power to Interdict whole Kingdoms;
that is, when they think the Rulers give them Cause; to
forbid the preaching of the Gospel and publick Worship of
God, to all the People of the Land; yea forbidding the
Clergie who are Subjects to obey their own Princes who
shall command them (as the Kings of* Israel *did the Priests
and Levites*) *to do their offices.*

That is, If the State or King offend them, they will
be avenged on God by denying him all Publick Worship, and on the souls of millions of innocent people by
doing their worst to send them to Hell, (where the un-
believing ignorant, and those that worship not God,
must go.) The instances in *Germany*, and the *Veneti-
an* Interdict and others are too full proof of their Claim
and Practice.

XII. *The Pope claimeth power, even by the Decrees of an
approved*

approved General Council to oblige all men to believe that all theirs and all other mens senses and perception upon sense, are certainly deceived, when they think that there is real Bread and Wine after Consecration: And this denyal of all mens Common sense, he hath made an Article of faith, and necessary to salvation.

XIII. He hath by the same Council decreed that all those that do not thus far renounce all their senses, shall be exterminated and made uncapable to make any will, &c. And by other of his Laws, that they be all burnt as Hereticks; and delivered to that end to the secular power.

XIV. By the same Council he hath decreed that Temporals Lords shall take an Oath to execute this Decree, and shall be excommunicated if they exterminate not all such Believers of sense from their dominions: And to dishonour Kings by Excommunications (whom the fifth Commandment bids us honour) is an act of Papal power.

XV. By the same Council he hath Decreed to depose all temporal Lords that will not thus destroy or exterminate their Subjects, and to give their Dominions to Papists that will do it: So that the Popes power to depose Princes is become an Article of their Religion.

And in his *Roman* Councils *Greg.* 7 declareth that he hath power to take down and set up Kings and Emperors: And in his Letters to the *German* Clergy: And what he said, he did practise by bloody and unnatural wars, to the great distraction of all the Empire.

Saith *Innocent* 3. Serm. 2. [" To me it is said, I have " set thee over Nations and Kingdoms, to set up and de- " stroy, and scatter-----I am set up as a middle person be- " tween God and Man; on this side God, but beyond Man; " yea greater than Man; who judge all, and can be judged " of none: I am the Bridegroom, &c.]

XVI. By

XVI. *By the same Council he hath power to dispense with the Oaths of all the Subjects of such Princes, and to disoblige them, how many soever, from their Allegiance; so that the Popes Power thus to dissolve the obligation of Oaths is also become an Article of their Religion.*

I prove all these together, by giving you the words of the Council in English. Once again (though I have oft cited them) *c.* 1. they say that [" No man can be saved " out of their Universal Church.] And *c.* 2. that [" The " Bread and Wine in the Sacrament of the Altar are tran-" substantiate into the Body and Blood of Christ, the " appearances remaining.] And *c.* 3. [" We excommu-" nicate and anathematize every Heresie extolling it self " against this holy Orthodox Catholick Faith, which we " have before expounded, condemning all Hereticks by " what Names soever they be called-----And being con-" demned, let them be left to the present Secular Power, " or their Bayliffs, to be punished, the Clergy being first " degraded of their Orders. And let the Goods of such " condemned ones be confiscate, if they be Lay-men; " but if they be Clergy-men, let them be given to the " Churches whence they had their Stipends. And those " that are found to be noted *only by suspicion*, if they do " not by congruous purgation demonstrate their inno-" cency, according to the considerations of the suspicion, " and the quality of the person, let them be smitten with " the Sword of Anathema, and avoided by all men, till they " have given sufficient satisfaction; and if they remain a " year excommunicate let them be condemned as Here-" ticks: And let the *Secular Powers, in what Office soever,* " be admonished and perswaded, and if it be necessary, " *compelled* by Ecclesiastical censure, that as they would " be reputed and accounted Believers, so for the defence
"of

" of the Faith, *they take an Oath publickly*, that they will
" study in good earnest, according to their power, to ex-
" terminate all that are by the Church denoted Hereticks,
" from the Countries subject to their jurisdiction. So
" that when *any one shall be taken into Spiritual* or *Tempo-*
" *ral Power*, he shall by *his Oath* make good this Chapter.
" But if the Temporal Lord, being admonished by the
" Church, shall neglect to purge his Country of hereti-
" cal defilement, let him by the Metropolitan, and other
" com-Provincial Bishops be tyed by the bond of Excom-
" munication. And if he refuse to satisfie within a year,
" let it be signified to the Pope, that he may from thence-
" forth denounce his Vassals absolved from his fidelity,
" and may expose his Country to be seized on by Ca-
" tholicks, who rooting out the Hereticks may possess it
" without contradiction, and may keep it in the purity
" of Faith, saving the Right of the Principal Lord, so
" be it that he himself do make no hindrance hereabout,
" nor oppose any impediment: And the same Law is to
" be observed with them that are not Principal Lords.
" And the Catholicks that, taking the Sign of the Cross,
" shall set themselves to the rooting out of the Hereticks,
" shall enjoy the same Indulgences and holy Priviledges
" which were granted to those that go to the relief of the
" Holy Land. Moreover we decree, That the Believers,
" Receivers, Defenders, and Favourers of Hereticks shall
" be Excommunicate; firmly decreeing, that after any
" such is noted by Excommunication, if he refuse to sa-
" tisfie within a year, he shall from thenceforth be *ipso*
" *jure, infamous*, and may not be admitted to publick
" Offices or Councils or to the choice of such, or to bear
" witness: And he shall be intestate, and not have pow-
" er to make a will, nor may come to a succession of In-
heritance:

"heritance: And no man shall be forced to answer him in "any Cause but he shall be forced to answer others: And "if he be a Judge, his sentence shall be invalid, and no "Causes shall be brought to his hearing: If a Notary (or "Register) the instruments made by him shall be utterly "void, and damned with the damned Author: And so "in other like cases we command that it be observed. They further command Bishops by themselves or their Archdeacons or other fit persons, once or twice a year to search every Parish where any Heretick is found to dwell, and to put all the Neighbourhood to their Oathes, whether they know of any Hereticks there, or of any *private meetings, or any that in life and manners do differ from the Common Conversation of the faithful, &c.* And the Bishops that neglect this are to be cast out, and others put into their places that will do them.

Here you see that no man must live on Earth (for all Kingdoms must be subject to the Pope) that will not renounce his humanity and animality or common senses, and declare himself below a Beast, That all Kings are the Popes Subjects, commanded by him, and must take a new Oath when they are crowned to destroy all their Subjects that believe their senses; That even the suspected are undone if they prove not the Negative: That Princes must be a thousand fold worse than hang-men, who hang not whole Countries but a few condemned Maleafctors: *T*hat Popes can and must depose Kings, and Lords that will not do such things as these, and give their Dominion to others: *T*hat the sign of the Cross is the Cross Makers sign: *T*hat all the promises of the pardon and happiness that were made to the invaders of the holy Land are given to those Wretches, that when they have lived in filthiness and wickedness will expiate it by murdering the innocent (as they did, say Historians, by above an hundred thousand.) This is the *Roman* way to heaven. That the very favorers of these men that will not renounce humanity are to be also utterly ruined. That (as in the *Japan* persecution of the Christians) all the neighbour-hood must be Sworn to detect them? And the office of a Bishop is to see all this done: And now if you *will see* you see how the Church of *Rome* is upheld, and propagated: And what the Religion called Popery is? And consider whether as Angels and Saints are near of Kin, or like in disposition, it be not so also with *Devils* and *wicked men*: And whether all Protestants be not Dead men in Law, or condemned, where the Papal Religion and Laws are received: And what will follow hereupon.

And besides *Gregory* the first's Declaration in his *Roman* Councils before mentioned, he saith in *Epist.* 7. l. 4. [" And for the conspiracy of Hereticks and the King, we " believe it is not unknown to you that are near them " how it may be impugned by the Catholick Bishops " and Dukes; and many others in the *German* parts.: " For the faithful of the Church of *Rome* are come to " such a number, that unless the King shall come to sa-" tisfaction, they may openly profess to chuse another " King; and observing Justice, we have promised " to favour them, and will keep our promise firm, " &c.

XVII. *The Pope, though pretending to be the infallible Judge of Controversies, doth tolerate his most famous Learned Doctors, in great numbers, without any Condemnation or disowning, to write that excommunicate Kings are no Kings, and may lawfully be killed, as some say by the Popes consent or direction, or as others say, without it.*

Henry

Henry Fowlis in his Book of *Popish Treasons*, hath so largely proved, by citing the *express words* of their chief Doctors, Jesuits, Dominicans and others, that this is their ordinary assertion, that I must remit the Reader thither for full satisfaction beyond all denyal.

I briefly refer you but to the words of Learned *Suarez advers. sect. Angl. l. 6. Cap. 4. sect. 14.* and *Cap. 6. sect. 22. 24. Azorius Instit. Mor. part.1.l.8.c.13.* And *Dom. Bannes in Thom.22. q. 12. a. 2.* saith ["*When there is evident knowledg of the Crime, Subjects may lawfully exempt themselves from the Power of their Princes, before any declaratory, sentence of a Judge, so they have but strength to do it.*] [Hence it followeth that the *faithful* (Papists) *of* England *and* Saxonie *are to be excused, that do not free themselves from the Power of their Superiours, nor make war against them: because commonly they are not strong enough, to manage those wars: and great dangers hang over them.*

So then, the disability of the Papists is all the security we can hope for from them.

Augustine Triumphus saith (*de potest. Eccl.* q. 46. a. 2.) "*There is no doubt but the Pope may depose all Kings, when there is reasonable cause for it.*

Part of *Suarez* words are (*Defens. fid. Cath.* l. 6. c. 4. §. 14.) ["*After sentence he is altogether deprived of his Kingdom, so that he cannot by just title possess it: Therefore from thence-forward he may be handled as a meer Tyrant, and consequently any private man may kill him.*

I have elsewhere cited *Card. Perrons* words out of Bishop *Usher* professing that, *if the Pope may not depose Kings, it will follow that he is Antichrist who hath so long professed it:* I grant the consequence.

XVIII. *The Pope professeth the fallibility of General Councils, but that he is infallible himself.*

The first is proved by his reprobating many. For the second, faith *Leo* 10. *in Bull. cont. Luth. in Bin.* p. 655. [" *The holy Popes our predecessours never erred in their Canons and Constitutions.*]

XIX. *They hold this gift of infallibility to be by supernatural Inspiration, beyond all natural faculties and means; even to men that cannot Read or have no Learning, at least none in the Text of Scripture, to judge of such Texts, the translation and exposition of them.*

That they pretend to be Judges in Controversies *de fide*, I need not prove: Nor that some have been Lads, and some Men unlearned, as I proved before of *Greg.* 6. Their own Histories agree in this.

XX. *Though the Decrees of General Councils be their very Religion, and pretended immutable, the Pope pretendeth to a Power to change them.* (And yet they pretend that all is old and from their forefathers.)

Both these foregoing parts are proved, by Pope *Julius* 2. in his General Council at the *Laterane* with their approbation, *Monitor. cont. Prag. Sanct. Bin.* Vol. 4. p. 560. [" *Though the Institutions of sacred Canons, holy Fathers, and Popes of Rome ----- and their Decrees be judged immutable as made by Divine Inspiration, yet the Pope of Rome, who though of unequal merits, holdeth the place of the Eternal King, and the Maker of all Things and all Laws on Earth, may abrogate these Decrees when they are abused.*

XXI. *By the same pretended Power he changeth Christs own Instituted Sacrament, even in the substance of it, denying all the Laity the Cup, while they condemn all that will not believe that the wine is turned into his very Blood; And he that eateth not the Flesh of Christ, and*
drinketh

drinketh not his Blood, hath not Life, (*which they expound of the Sacrament.*)

Chrift faid when he had given them the Cup, *Drink yes all of it, Mat.* 26. 27. And *Paul* delivereth it to the *Laity* from the Lord, 1 Cor. 11. 23. 25. 28. [" This do " ye, as oft as ye drink it, in remembrance of me.] " And [as oft as ye eat this Bread, and drink this Cup, " ye fhew the Lords death till he come: Let a man exa-" mine himfelf, and fo let him eat of this Bread, and " drink of this Cup] 1 *Cor.* 10. 21. Ye cannot drink " the Cup of the Lord, and the Cup of Devils, is gi-" ven to the Laity as a reafon againft their Idol Commu-" nion. In relation to the Sacrament it's faid that [all " were made to drink into one Spirit.] The recepti-on of the Spirit being likened to that drinking. And if the Pope may abrogate one half the Sacrament, why not the other.

XXII. *The Pope declareth all the world to be damned except his own Subjects.*

See the forefaid firft Canon of *Innocents Laterane* Council.

Leo 10. *Abrog. Pragm. Sanct. Bul. in the* 17. General Council at *Laterane* faith [" *And feeing it is of neceffity* " *to falvation that all the faithful of Chrift be fubject to the* " *Pope of* Rome, *as we are taught by the Teftimony of* " *Divine Scripture and of the holy Fathers, and it is de-* " *clared in the conftitution of Pope* Boniface *the* 7. &c.

Pope *Pius* 2. was converted from the fupremacie of Councils by this Doctrine of a Cardinal which he ap-proveth (or by the Popedom,) *Bul. Retract. in Bin. Vol.* 4. *p.* 514. [" I came to the Fountain of truth which the " holy Doctors both Greek and Latine fhew, who with " one Voice fay, that he cannot be faved that holdeth
" not

"not the Unity of the holy Church of *Rome*; and that
"all those Virtues are maimed to him that refuseth to
"obey the Pope of *Rome*; though he lye in Sackcloth
"and Ashes, and fast and pray both Day and Night, and
"seem in the rest or other things to fulfil the Law of
"God.

(*Bellarmine* saith *de Eccles. l. 3. c. 5.*) that ["No man,
"though he would, can be subject to Christ, that is not
"subject to the Pope.] And therefore he saith that our
Baptism implicitely subjecteth us to the Pope; or we
are so baptized to him.

And saith *Gonzal. Rodericus in Godignus de rebus Abassin.* l. 2. c. 18. p. 323. to the Emperours Mother, [*I denyed that any one is subject to Christ that is not subject to his Vicar.*] But said the old Woman to him, [*Neither I nor mine do deny obedience to S.* Peter: *we are in the same Faith now that we were in from the beginning: If that was not the right, why was there no one found in so many Ages and Generations that would warn us of our Errour?*] (See here what Tradition is, and whether the Papal Church and Charge was Universal.) The Jesuite answered, [*The Pope of* Rome *who is Pastor of the whole Church of Christ, could not in the years that are by-past send Teachers into* Abassia, *because the* Mahometans *incompassed all, and had left no passage to them; but now the Maritime way to* Æthiopia *is open, they can do that which they could not do before.*]

So that it seemeth, 1. Christ hath made the Pope Governour of Countries that he cannot send to, and set the poor man an impossible task. 2. He hath made it necessary to salvation to whole Kingdoms to believe in a Pope that they could never hear from; nor whether there were such a Man or City in the world. 3. Or else
their

their Faith groweth new as the Sea paſſage is open. And wo to them if their new acquaintance with the Pope make all, all, all his Laws neceſſary to them, which they might have been ſaved without before. How much happier were they when they never heard of his Name?

See here, all you Jeſuites, one old Woman is able unanſwerably to confute you all, if ſhe ſtand but on equal ground with you, and be not under your power, inquiſition, or fear.

XXIII. *In ſo doing the Pope damneth and unchurcheth about two or three parts of the Chriſtians upon earth, and ſo would deſtroy the Body Politick of Chriſt.*

For the Body is rather to be denominated from the greater part than from the leſs: Elſe why do Votes in General Councils go for the ſenſe of the Church? And I have ſhewed before that the *Abaſſines, Copties* in *Egypt, Syrians, Armenians, Georgians, Greeks, Moſcovites, Proteſtants*, and the reſt, are far more (two or three to one) than all the Papiſts in the World. Much more when *Mahometaniſm* had not drowned ſo many Countries that were of the *Greek* Profeſſion, was it ſo.

And how the Saviour of the World will take it for this Uſurper to rob him of the moſt of his Flock, and damn moſt of his Church, (and corrupt the reſt) conſider and judge.

XXIV. *By ſo doing the Pope ſets a Sect, or ſmall divided Parcel of the Church, and calleth it the whole Church of Chriſt.*

Even as ſome Anabaptiſts (I hope not many) and other Sects appropriate Chriſtianity, or true Church-Communion, *to themſelves,* and ſay, *we are all the Church!* ſo doth the Pope: His Univerſal Church is *too ſmall* for any underſtanding Chriſtian to own, as ſuch, and to be a Member of, as ſuch.   XXV. *The*

XXV. *The Pope damneth not only two or three parts of the Christian World, but also his own Representative Body, or Church, called Papists ; such an Abaddon is he.*

Proved. The General Councils at *Constance* and *Basil* (to say nothing of many others) were the Representative Church of the Papists, and took it to be *de fide that a Council was above the Pope*: But the Pope hath damned them for this as an error, and for their deposing Popes: See *Concil. Later. sub Jul.* 2. and *sub Leone* 10. & *Concil. Florent.* Review the fore-cited Speeches of *Cajetan* and *Pighius* against them. Many more Councils have they condemned.

XXVI. *Yea Popes have damned Popes also,* (*and it is most to be feared lest they damn themselves, more than others.*)

I need not tell of *Marcellinus*, nor of *Honorius* condemned for an Heretick by divers Popes ; nor repeat the Schismes and Damnations of each other therein, nor the Story of *Sergius* and *Formosus* and *Stephen, &c.* nor their forementioned wickedness. *Watson* in his *Quodlibets* tells you of *Bellarmines* Sentence against *Pope Sixtus Quintus*, [*Conceptis verbis, quantum capio, quantum sapio, quantum intelligo, Dominus noster Papa descendit ad infernum* :] And as others report him [*Qui sine pœnitentia vivit, & sine pœnitentia moritur, ad infernum descendit.*] See *Baronius* forecited.

XXVII. *Though the Pope condemn and unchurch so many, yet doth he tolerate in his own Church abundance of differences, de fide, and abundance of Controversies in Theologie, and abundance of Differences and Errours in great and dangerous matters of Morality, and abundance of Sects that variously serve God, so they will serve him, and uphold his Kingdom.*

1. The

1. The holy Scripture is all *de fide*, that is, a Divine Revelation to be believed: The Popes tolerated Translations that differ in many hundred places, or that *erred* so oft; and *Commentators* that differ in many hundred Texts as to the *Exposition*; yea, they tolerate those that deny the immaculate conception of the Virgin, after a General Council hath defined it.

2. He tolerateth vast Volumes of Theological Differences, in the School Doctors.

3. He tolerateth all the *Moral Doctrines* for *murdering Kings* before mentioned, and all those cited by Mr. *Clarkson* in his *Practical Divinity of the Church of Rome*, and all those mentioned in the Provincial Letters, and the Jesuites Morals, about Murder, Adultery, Perjury, Lying, seldom loving God, not loving him intensively above all, &c. See my *Key*, &c. *p.* 59.

4. He tolerateth abundance of Religious Sects, Jesuites, *Augustinians, Franciscans, Carthusians*, &c. who differ from each other in their serving God, as much as many of the Sects of Protestants, who are despised for their discord.

XXVIII. *He pretendeth a necessity to the ending of Controversies that he be the Judge, and yet will not end them by his Judgment, but continueth many hundred undecided.*

If we dispute with a Papist, and cite the Scriptures, they ask us presently, *who shall be Judge of the meaning of them*? As if the Pope would decide all: And yet to this day he will neither write any deciding Commentary on the Bible, nor on one Book of it; nor end the Controversies among his own Commentators. Nor will he end any of the fore-mentioned Controversies in *Morality*, of great importance.

XXIX. *He sweareth all his Clergie never to take or interpret Scripture, but according to the unanimous sense of the Fathers,* (see the *Trent* Oath:) *when yet the Fathers do not unanimously expound the Scripture, nor any one Book of it.*

And few Priests know what the Fathers are unanimous in, nor can do, unless they read them all; which by this Oath they seem obliged to do. Was not *Greg. Nazianz.* one of the Fathers? who saith, *Orat.* 18. ["I would there were no Presidency, nor Prerogative of place, and tyrannical Priviledges; that so we might be known only by Vertue, (or deserts:) But now this Right side and Left side, and Middle and Lower Degree, and Presidency and Concomitancy, have begot us many contentions to no purpose, and have driven many into the Ditch, and have led them away to the Region of Goats.] Is not this Heresie, or worse, with you?

Was not *Isidore Pelusiota* a Father? (but a sharp Reprover of proud and wicked Priests and Prelates) who saith, *lib.* 3. *Epist.* 223. *ad Hieracem* [" And when I have shewed what difference there is between the ancient Ministry and the present Tyranny, why do you not crown and praise the lovers of Equality?] Doth not this deserve a Fagot with you?

How ordinarily doth *Cajetan,* and others of yours, reject (deservedly) the Expositions of Fathers? *Bellarmine* chargeth *Justin, Irenæus, &c.* with error, *de Beat. SS. li.* 1. *Cap.* 6. He saith, [*There is no trust to be given to* Tertullian, *de Rom. Pont. li.* 4. *c.* 8. He saith, *Eusebius* was addicted to *Hereticks, and that* Cyprian *seemed to sin mortally, de Rom. Pont. li.* 4. *c.* 7. *Dionys. Petavius de Trinit.* citeth the words of most of the ancientest

cienteſt as favouring Arrianiſm (almoſt like *Sondius* himſelf or *Philoſtorgius*;) and is fain to go to the [*Major Vote of the Nicene Council as the proof*,] that moſt of the ancients were not really of the *Arrians* mind. *Dallæus* hath told you more of the Fathers differences, and unſatisfactory expoſitions.

XXX. *He confeſſeth all the Scripture to be Gods infallible word, yea his Doctors have aſſerted its ſufficiency as a Divine Law; and yet his pretenſe of its Inſufficiency without Traditional ſupplement, is one of the Pillars of his Kingdom.*

The ſecond part needs no proof: For the firſt, the elder Popes oft aſſert it; And the School-men in their Prologue to the Sentences (*Scotus, Durandus* and many others:) But when Reformers confuted them by Scripture, they found that would not ſerve their turn, (as *Micaiah* of *Ahab,* it propheſyed not good of them but evil.) And ſince then, they cry up the *Church* and *Tradition,* and depreſs the ſufficiency of Scripture.

Even *Card. Richlieu pag.* 38. confeſſeth ["As for us, "we aſſert no other Rule but Scripture, neither of ano-"ther ſort, nor total: yea we ſay that it is the whole "Rule of our ſalvation, and that on a double account: "both becauſe it containeth immediately and formally "the ſum of our ſalvation; that is, all the Articles that "are neceſſary to mans ſalvation, by neceſſity of means; "and becauſe it mediately containeth what ever we "are bound to believe, as it ſends us to the Church to be "inſtructed by her, of whoſe infallibility it certainly con-"firmeth us.] ⸺ Here the ſum of our Religion is granted.

At the Council of *Baſil Raguſius*'s oration (*Bin. p.* 299) ſaith ["That Faith and all things neceſſary to ſalvation, "both matters of belief and practice, are founded in the "literal

"literal sense of Scripture, and only from that may ar-
"gumentation be taken for the proving of those things
"that are matters of Faith and necessary to salvation,
"and not from those passages that are spoken by allego-
"ry, &c. And *sup.* 7. ["The holy Scripture in the li-
"teral sense soundly and well understood, is the infallible
"and most sufficient rule of Faith."] See more of his oration opened in my *Key pag.* 93, 94, 95. The Testimony of
Bellarmine, Costerus and others I have formerly recited.

XXXI. *The Pope teacheth us that we cannot truly believe the Articles of our Faith or the truth of Scripture, but
because of the Authority and Infallibility of the Pope and his
Church declaring them; so that we must believe that the
Pope is Chrifts Vicar and authorized by him, and made infallible, before we can believe that there is a Chrift, or
that he hath given any authority or gifts to any.*

This is not to be denyed: And *Knot* against *Chillingworth* hath no other shift, but to resolve their belief of
the Churches infallibility and authority, not into any
word or donation of Christ, but into *Miracles wrought by
the Church.* So that no man can be a Believer that is
not first certain of the Papists Miracles (and how can
millions know them, when they see them not? and in
all my life I could never meet with one that saw them.)
And he must next be certain that those miracles prove
the infallibility of the Pope; when yet they confess that
they prove not the Infallibility of him *that doth them.*
Valentine <u>Greatreaky</u> hath done and still doth more won-
derous cures by *touch* or *stroaking,* than ever I heard
by any credible report that any Papist did: and yet he
pretendeth to no Infallibility.

And those Canonized Saints that have been most credibly famed for the greatest Miracles, have born their
Testimony

Testimony against Popery, and therefore Popery was not confirmed by them. For instance, St. *Martin* is by his Disciple and Friend *Sulpitius Severus* affirmed to have done more Miracles than I have ever credibly read done by any since the Apostles: I scarce except *Gregory Neocæsar*: And yet, whereas the Papal Councils give high priviledges, of pardon, *&c.* to those that will take the Cross to kill the *Waldenses*, and compel Princes to it, and uphold their Kingdom by such means, St. *Martin* separated to the death from the Synods and Bishops about him, for seeking the Magistrates Sword to be drawn against even *Priscillian Gnosticks*, and he professeth that an *Angel* appeared to him and chastised him sharply for once communicating with the Bishops at the motion of *Maximus*, when he did it only to save mens lives, that were condemned as *Priscillianists.* Here are Miracles against the very Pillars of Popery.

So also the *Egyptian* Monks were the most famous for Miracles of any People. And yet (as their Miracles were no confirmation of the errour of the *Anthropomorphites* which their simplicity and rashness involved them in, so) they renounced Communion with the Church of *Rome*, and therefore confirmed it not by their Miracles.

How few Christians be there on Earth, if none are such but those that by known Popish miracles believed the Pope to be infallible before they believed that there was a Christ?

And thus they must believe him to be Infallible not as Pope, but somewhat else: For to be Pope, is to be [*Christs pretended Vicar:*] And to believe that he is authorized or Infallible as *Christs Vicar*, before they believe there is a *Christ*, is a mad-mans contradiction and impossible.

ble. What Infallible wight then is it that we muſt firſt believe the Pope to be, before we believe him to be Pope? To what impudence will intereſt and faction carry men?

I will again recite the words of an honeſt Jeſuit, *Joſeph. Acoſta de tempor. noviſ. li. 3. c. 3.* [" To all the " miracles of Antichriſt, though he do great ones, the " Church ſhall boldly oppoſe the belief of the Scriptures: " And by the inexpugnable teſtimony of this truth, ſhall " by moſt clear light expel all his juglings as Clouds ---- " Signs are given to Infidels ; Scriptures to Believers ; " and therefore the primitive Church abounded with " miracles, when Infidels were to be called : But the " laſt, when the faithful are already called, ſhall reſt more " on the Scripture than on miracles: yea I will boldly " ſay, that all miracles are vain and empty, unleſs they " be approved by the Scripture ; that is, have a Do-" ctrine conform to the Scripture. But the Scripture " it ſelf is of it ſelf a moſt firm argument of truth.

Obj. " But he grants that Infidels had miracles. *Anſ.* He lived long in the *Weſt-Indies* among them, and in his *Treat.* of the *Converſ. Ind.* and his *Hiſt. Ind.* he profeſſeth that the Ignorance, Drunkenneſs and Wickedneſs of the Roman Prieſts there, was the great hinderance of their Converſion ; but that *Miracles* there were none. God had not given them there any ſuch gift.

Once more, Did the Miracle which *Thyræus de Dæmoniacis,* p. 76. reciteth out of *Proſper,* that [*A perſon poſſeſſed by the Devil was cured by drinking the wine in the Euchariſt*] confirm the Popes Religion, who hath caſt out the Cup ; or the Proteſtants that uſe it ?

XXXII. *Though S. Paul ſay, Let every Soul be ſubject to*

to the higher *Powers*, and give honour to whom honour is due, the *Pope* as far as he is able exempteth all his *Clergie* from the Government of the *Magiſtrate*; yea they are forbidden to fall down to *Princes*, or eat at their Tables, but *Emperours* muſt take them as equals.

The firſt part is commonly known: *Caranz.* pag. 395. reciteth this Decree of Pope *Nicholas*, that ["No Lay "man muſt judge a Prieſt, nor examine any thing of his "life: And no Secular Prince ought to judge the facts of "any Biſhops or Prieſts whatſoever.

The Eighth General Council at *Conſtantinople* faith, *Can.* 14. [" Miniſters muſt not fall down to Princes, nor "eat at their Tables, nor debaſe themſelves to them; "but Emperours muſt take them as equals.

XXXIII. *The Pope confeſſeth every word of our Objective Religion to be true; for all his killing and damning us as Hereticks.*

Proved before: We have not a word of our Objective Religion, but the Sacramental Covenant, and its Expoſition in the *Creed*, *Lords Prayer*, and *Decalogue*, and the *Canonical Scripture*, which we receive. And they confeſs all this to be infallibly true, and ſo juſtifie all our Poſitive Religion.

XXXIV. *The Popes to this day will not tell the Church ſo much as what a Chriſtian is, and what muſt make a man a Member of their Church, in the Eſſentials of a Member.* Of which more anon.

XXXV. *While the Decrees of General Councils are made* quoad nos *the Churche's Faith, the Pope will never let us know how big our Faith muſt be, nor when we ſhall have all.*

If every General Council add new Articles (or many) quoad nos; who knoweth when they will have
done?

done? and whether we have yet half the Christian Faith, or not?

XXXVI. *The Popes Religion maketh Contradictions necessary to be believed*; that is, *impossibilities*.

The Contradictions of *Transubstantiation* I have opened in my [*Full Satisfaction*] Confirmed General Councils they commonly agree do make Decrees which must necessarily be believed: And it is notorious, that such Decrees are Contradictory. The General Council at *Constance* confirmed by *Martin* 5. and that at *Basil* confirmed by *Fælix* 5. do make it *de fide* for a Council to be above the Pope. *Bin. p. 43. 79. 96. Conc. Basil. Sess. ult.* they say, [" Not one of the skilful did ever doubt, but " that the Pope was subject to the judgment of a Gene- " ral Council in matters of Faith; and that he cannot " without their consent dissolve or remove a General " Council; yea and that this is an Article of Faith, which " without destruction of salvation cannot be denied, and " that *de fide* the Council is above the Pope, and that he " is a Heretick that is against this.] *Eugenius* also owned this Council, *Bin. ib. p. 42.*

But the Councils of *Florence*, and at the *Laterane sub Jul.* 2. and *sub Leone* 10. say the clean contrary.

The 6. Council at *Constant*. approved by Pope *Adrian* is now said by them to have many errors.

XXXVII. *The Pope arrogateth power to alter the constitutions of the Spirit of God in the holy Scriptures.*

Proved. The Council of *Constance* taking away the Cup saith [" Though in the Primitive Church this Sa- " crament was received by Believers under both " kinds, &c.] yea though Christ so instituted it, yet they altered it.

I elsewhere cited Pope *Innocents* words [*By the fulness of of our Power we can dispense with the Law, being above the Law.*] And the Gloss oft saith, [*The Pope dispenseth against the Apostle, against the Old Testament, &c.*

The Council of *Trent* say, *Sess.* 21. *cap.* 1, 2. that [*This power was always in the Church, that in dispensing the Sacraments, saving the substance of them, it may ordain or change things as it should judge most expedient to the profit of the Receiver.* (But is not the Cup of the substance, as truly as the Bread?)

Andrad. Def. Conc. Trid. li. 2. *p.* 236. ["Hence it is "plain that they do not erre that say, the Popes of *Rome* "may sometimes dispense with Laws made by *Paul*, and "the four first Councils. And *Vasquez* saith *To.* 2. *Disp.* 216. *N.* 60. ["Though we grant that this was a Pre- "cept of the Apostles, yet the Church and Popes might "on just causes abrogate it: For the power of the Apo- "stles was no greater than the power of the Church and "Pope in bringing in Precepts.]

One of *Luthers* Opinions opposed as Heretical by *Leo* 10. was this, [*It is certain that it is not in the hand of the Church or Pope to make Articles of Faith.*] See more in my *Key*, *p.* 243, 244.

XXXVIII. *The Pope setteth up a Publick worship of God, in a Tongue not understood by most of the worshippers; and forbiddeth men, without Licence to read the Scriptures in a known Tongue.*

Practice and the *Trent* Council prove both these.

XXXIX. *The Pope determineth that the Image of Christ be reverenced with equal honour as the holy Scriptures.*]

So it is decreed *Concil. Constant.* the eighth *General Can.* 3. And yet Images are mans work, and at the best unnecessary, and the holy Scriptures are Gods work by his Spirit, and the Law by which we must live, and be judged at the last. XL. *And*

XL. *And when all this Power over the whole Earth is thus claimed, there is no possible means left for any mortal man, much less for the* Antipodes, *to know who is the man that hath this Power, and whom on pain of damnation we must obey, and believe in before we can believe in* Christ.

Proved: If there be any possibility of knowing it, it must be either, 1. By personal qualifications of mind; 2. Or by right of election; 3. Or of Ordination; 4. Or of Possession; 5. Or of Acceptance by the Church after Possession. I cannot Imagine any other way. But there is no possibility of knowing who is Pope by any of *these wayes*.

I. The first is not pretended by them: But anon we shall thence prove their *Nullity* for want of necessary Qualifications.

II. If *Election* will tell us, then it is either *any Election whatsoever*, or else *Election by authorized Persons*. Not the first; else the *Turks*, or the *Greeks*, or the Adversaries of *Rome* might elect a Pope: And an hundred might be elected at once several ways. Not the later; For if any *one way of Election* be necessary, Popes were no Popes when that way failed: Sometime they were elected by the *People of Rome* (and were *they* the Chusers for *all the world*?) Sometimes by the People and the *Presbyters*: Sometimes by the *Neighbour Bishops* and Ordainers: Sometimes by the Emperours: And lastly by the Cardinals. If one way only be valid, the rest were invalid: And how shall we prove which? If any of these ways are valid; then six men or five may be chosen at once by the several ways: And where is the proof?

III. If *Ordination* be the notifying Title, then, 1. Those Lay men that were put in full possession unordained were no no Popes; and where then is the Succession? 2. And who is it that hath that *ordaining Authority*? If some Bishops ordain one, and some another, and so twenty (as they long did divers in many years Schism) which of these is the true Pope? or is it *all*?

IV. If *Possession* were the Title, then the *Turk* may be Pope; or he that can get it by the Sword: Then there can be no Usurper, but the strongest hath best Right. Then he that kept at *Rome* had better title than he that was in *Germany*, or at *Avignion*.

V. If it be the Churches *after acceptance*; then, 1. He was an Usurper before. 2. And what or who is that *Accepting Church*? Sure they that must make a Pope of no Pope, by after acceptance, should have the antecedent Election: Else Popes must all be first Usurpers, before they are true Popes. But, 1. If it must be the *major part* of the *Christian world*, then there is no Pope, because two parts are against him. If it must be one Sect of Christians only like the Papists, that will but think themselves the Church, or better than the rest; who is it that can prove their title to this Choice? And must it be *All of them*, or but *Part*? If *All*, 1. How shall we ever know it? Never such a thing was tryed. 2. And then there was no Pope in the 40 or 50 years Schism. If it must be *Part*, how shall we ever know *which part* it must be? If the *major* or the *melior*, how shall it be ever tryed and known in a division? None to this day knoweth who had the *major* or *melior* part in many a Schism.

If they say that *silent non-opposition* is *Consent*. I Answer, That's a known Falshood, when most men, even a thousand to one, have neither Call nor Opportunity to signifie their dissent effectually; and when no wise men that love their time and peace, will run to *Rome* by thousands out of all Kingdoms, to tell them their diffent.

2. But it was no *silent submission*, when *several Popes* were upheld by *several Kingdoms*. So that there is no way of certain notice who is the true Pope, but he muſt go for the man, as *Eugenius* 4. did after his Depoſition, who can keep poſſeſſion, which is no title at all.

2. Yea, I prove certainly, according to their own Principles, that *there is no Pope* at *Rome*, nor *hath been* for many an hundred years.

For they hold themſelves, that the Right muſt be derived by an uninterrupted Succeſſion from S. *Peter*, (and call us no Miniſters for want of Succeſſion:) But that they have no ſuch uninterrupted Succeſſion is notorious.

For, 1. An Infidel and Heretick Pope, ſo openly judged, can be no Pope: Elſe a *Turk* might be Pope. For he that is no Chriſtian, is no Chriſtian Biſhop. But Popes (before mentioned) have been judged Infidels, Hereticks, incarnate Devils.

2. A Pope actually depoſed as an uncapable wicked Heretick, by a General Council, was no Pope: Yet ſuch was *Eugenius* 4. who yet kept the place, and the reſt are his Succeſſors.

3. There have been ſometimes ſeveral years without any Pope at all: And if two or three years make no interruption, how ſhall we know how long time doth it?

4. *Baronius, Genebrard*, and others aforementioned, confeſs that for 50 of them together they were Apoſtatical, and deſerve not to be named among the Popes, being wicked men, made and ruled by Whores, *&c.* Where then is the ſucceſſion?

And if it were poſſible for thoſe at *Rome* to know that there is a Pope, and to know who and which is he, yet

how

how should all the rest of the world have any assurance of it? You'll say, it is not necessary: Possession and common Report must satisfie them in *China*, *Congo*, *Abassia*, and the *Phillipines*, &c.

Answ. No Building can be stronger than its Foundation, nor Conclusion than its Premises: How then shall such men have assurance of their Religion when they must take it on the Credit of a Pope as infallible of whom they have no assurance? And how shall they be certain that they are of the right Church, when they are uncertain who is the Head whom they must be subjects to?

CHAP. VII.

What a PAPIST *is*.

II. HAving shewed *what a Pope is*, I am next hence to tell you what we Protestants take a *Papist* to be.

And first as to the *name*, it is equivocal: There are so many sorts that are called commonly by the one name of *Papists*, that it is hard to enumerate and describe them all.

1. There are some that believe that the *Pope* is but a *Humane Creature*, that hath run up his power into Tyranny by abuse, and it were well if he were either down, or reduced to his first state: But they take themselves to be as those that live under other abusive, oppressing or tyrannical Governours, who must live in Patience and Submission, and are not bound to ruine themselves, by opposing him in vain; and though he impose on them
many

many things which they like not, but had rather they were reformed, yet it being not in their power, and Princes and Magistrates commanding them the same, they take *Conformity* to be orderly, and *Nonconformity* to be unpeaceable and of ill fame; And if any of the things commanded them prove sinful, they hope God will forgive them (for bowing in the house of *Rimmon*) and will lay it on Popes, Princes and Prelates, and not on them that are not bound to study Controversies; and who do what they do but in obedience and for peace (pretenses that quiet their Consciences in self-saving Conformity:) I verily think that the greater part of those called Papists in all the world, are of this *self-saving sort*. As we see in all Countries that the greater number are or seem to be of the Religion of those in power, be it what it will be. And we ordinarily hear that the common people will thus talk against the Popes Doctrines and Practices, and yet quiet themselves on such terms of *Conformity* as I here describe.

II. Another sort called Papists do believe that the Pope is a meer humane creature also, not over all the world but in the Empire and where Princes let him: And consequently as men set him up, men might take him down. But yet that it is an *Orderly* Institution, as Kings and Emperors, and that his place is *Lawful*, and that it is the duty of the Church to obey him, especially when Princes also do command it: And that men have power from God to make, as *National*, *Provincial*, and *Patriarchal Churches* and *Rulers*, so also an *Universal Church* and *Ruler for Order and Unity sake* over many Countries, and that it is good and desirable to these ends.

Of these there are two sorts. 1. One sort take the
Papacie

Papacie and *Patriarchs* to be a lawful and laudable inſtitution of *Conſtantine*, confirmed by other Princes. 2. The other ſort take them to be laudable Inſtitutions of *General Councils*, or elſe of *particular conſenting Biſhops* before the firſt General Council (whom thy call the *Church*.)

III. Another ſort called Papiſts, do believe the Pope (as the former) to be a *humane Creature*, *viz.* of the firſt or ancient Biſhops by mutual conſent; but that it was a *neceſſary thing*, which by Gods General Laws, and his ſpecial Inſpiration, they did well, and were bound to do for the Churches concord and ſtrength; and that it is not lawful for the Church now to alter it, or any Prince in his Dominions.

Theſe alſo are of three ſorts: 1. Some think that the *Roman* Seat may be altered, and the Church upon juſt cauſe may remove the Primacy to another Biſhop. This ſeemeth to be the opinion of Cardinal *Cuſanus* afore cited *de Concord.* who ſaith, The Church might make the Biſhop of *Trent* chief. 2. Others ſeem rather to think, that God hath by Decree annexed the Supremacy to *Rome*, and yet (as *R. Smyth*, the Biſhop of *Calcedon*, and Ruler of the *Engliſh* Popiſh Clergy afore cited) think, that it is not *de fide*, that the Pope is *Peters* Succeſſor. 3. Others ſay that they are not ſure but *God* may deſtroy *Rome*, and remove the Primacy; but *Men* may not do it.

IV. The whole *Greek* Church ſeem yet of the ſecond or third opinion, (that the Pope had a juſt Primacy in one Empire, which was juſtly removed to *Conſtantinople*:) But there are ſome that think the Pope had alſo a juſt Primacy in all the *Chriſtian World*, and yet that he hath it but by *Humane Inſtitution*.

V. There are other that think the Pope is the Univerſal

sal Head by *Divine Institution*; even as S. *Peter*'s Successor, by derivation of the Power which Christ gave *Peter*.

And as about the *Foundation*, so about the *Subject* and the *Measure* of Power, yea *who is the true Chief Ruler* over the Uuniversal Church, there are these several sorts of Popery.

I. Some believe that it is *General Councils* that are the Subject or Possessors of *Supreme Church Power* and *Infallibility*, and that the Pope is but the first in order of the five Patriarchs in such *Councils*; who hath no necessary right to call them, nor no negative Voice in them, nor any Government over the other Patriarchs, or their Churches; but only the first Seat, if he be there; just as the Patriarch of *Alexandria* first, and of *Constantinople* after had when the Patriarch of *Rome* was absent. And thus indeed it was in the Empire, for a long time. But those five Patriarchs ruled not *all the World*; no more than our two Provincial Archbishops do.

II. Others called Papists do go farther, and believe that General Councils indeed have the supreme Legislative Power, and the chief Executive while they sit, and are the Seat of Infallibility: But because they are not to be *always* or *ordinary*, God hath not left the *four Patriarchs*, and *all the World*, ungoverned in the Intervals; but the *Roman* Pope is the *Supreme Governour of the World*, when there is no General Council: Yet so that he must Govern by *their Laws* or Canons.

III. Another sort (and I think the most numerous among the Learned) called Papists, hold that *Neither the Pope alone, nor the Council alone, are the Seat or Possessors of the supreme Legislative Power, or the Infallibility, nor of the supreme judging and executive power*

sedente

sedente concilio; *but it is both of them agreeing* or conjunct: And two Fallibles joyning, become one Infallible.

IV. Another sort of Papists, and very numerous especially in *Italy*, hold, that the Pope alone is Supreme and Infallible in Legislation and *Judgment*, and that Councils are but his Counsellors, to prepare Laws, to which his *Fiat* giveth *Authority and Infallibility*.

All these indeed are commonly called PAPISTS, because that more or less they are Subjects of the Pope. But who can give *one definition*, or the same *marks* of men that are really of so many minds? If I describe one sort, the other will say, this is not our Opinion; you do us wrong. And so of all the rest.

And here you may see, that when the Question is, *whether a Papist may be saved?* and *whether a Papist be a Heretick?* or the like; that it cannot be well answered, till we know of which sort of Papists you speak.

But because I find that already my Writing is swelled beyond my first intent, I will give you the Properties or *inadequate conceptions* of only one sort of Papists, which is the third sort in the last distribution, who hold the *Soveraignty and Infallibility to be in the Pope and Council conjunct, and that by Divine Right*: Because if I speak of any of the other sorts, I find they fly for refuge hither, and most Writers go upon this ground, and will own nothing as their Religion but what is in *Approved General Councils*.

And here I desire the Reader to peruse what I have said in my [*Full and easie satisfaction, &c.*] out of *Veron*, and others, as they describe their Faith themselves.

I. *A PAPIST of this sort is one that believeth that the Pope and his Council, or Church, is Infallible in proposing the*

the will of Christ; and believeth in Christ, and receiveth the Gospel as true, for the Authority and Infallibility of this Pope and Council, and hereon layeth all the hopes of his salvation, as on the Churches Faith: And all this Authority and Infallibility he believeth before he believeth that there is a Pope or a Church of Christ, or a Christ indeed, or a promise or gift from Christ of any Authority or Infallibility to them: Much more before he knoweth who is the true Pope, and which are true General Councils, or whether ever there were any such, or what it is that they have decreed to be believed.

1. That they take all their Faith in Christ and the Gospel on the credit of the Church (that is, the Pope and Council) proposing it, the moderatest of all this sort profess; as out of *Veron*, and others, I proved as aforecited. Hence it is that one tells us that the Scripture is so full of seeming Contradictions and Improbabilities, that he would no more believe it than *Esop*'s Fables, were it not for the Authority of the Church. Another said [Would I ever believe the Trinity, the Incarnation, that if you lay a man to dye in a close Chest of Lead or Marble his Soul could get out to Heaven, that the Body shall rise again, &c. were it not for the Authority of the Church?]

2. They believe this Infallibility and Authority of the *Pope* before they can believe that there is any Pope at all. For to be a *Pope* is essentially to be *Christs Vicar* as they describe him: And, as I said, it is impossible to believe that *Christ hath a Vicar*, before they believe that he is *Christ*. As it is to believe a *Son* without a Parent.

3. They believe the *Infallibility* and *Authority* of the *Church*, (as they profess) before they believe that there is any *Church*: For to be a *Church* is essentially to be a
Society

Society of *Christians*: And he that yet believeth not that *Christ* is truly *Christ*, cannot believe that *Christians* are truly *Christians*, save *de nomine*; nor that *Christ* hath a Church: For they are Relatives, as *Wife* and *Husband*.

4. They *believe* the *Infallibility* and *Authority* of the *Church*, that is, the Pope and *Council*, before they believe that *Jesus is the Christ*; For they profess to believe in him, because of the said Churches Authority and Infallibility: And the Premises go before the Conclusion.

5. They believe the said Infallibility and Authority of the Church, before they believe that ever *Christ gave* them such *Authority* and *Infallibility*: For they cannot believe that Christ gave it them, before they believe that there is a *Christ*, and a *word of gift*.

And now is not here a Riddle hard enough to pose the wisest? *which way do all these Believers, through all the world, come to know that the Pope and Council, or Church, are authorized and Infallible, before they believe that Christ ever gave it them? which way do they think that they came by it?* Let him unriddle it that can.

6. They believe thus in the Pope, before they know *what a Pope is*, or *who is he* that they must thus believe in. For alas, how can all or any in the world know what is necessary to make a Pope? what *Election*? what *Ordination*? what *Qualification*? and whether the man *had* all these? And of divers Pretenders *which is he* that hath the proofs of a true title?

7. They believe thus in *Councils*, when they know not what *Councils* are true, and what not; nay whether ever there were any: For I have elsewhere fully proved that there never was any, nor ever will be, that are truly Universal as to all the Christian World.

8. Much

8. Much less do these beginners know certainly, what General Councils have decreed to be believed by those that will be saved.

That which will be said to all this is, that *It is not necessary that all men receive their Faith from Councils; it is sufficient if it be from the Church-real, though not from the Representative.*

Ans. Very good: 1. Else no man was a Christian, nor could be, before the first General Council, which was above 300 years.

2. But still this answereth none of the Contradictions about believing in and from the *Pope*: May we all take our Faith from the Church-real, without taking it from the Pope, or not? If *yea*, we may possibly be good friends at last. If *not*, all the Contradictions about him are still upheld by you.

3. And if you must take it from the *Authority* and *Infallibility* of the *Church Real*, still all the Contradictions will follow as if you took it from *Councils*: For can you believe that this Church is *Christs Church*, and hath this power and gift from him, before you believe that he is Christ, and that ever he made such a gift or promise to them?

4. And *who* or *what* is this *Real Church*, that must be *first known* to be thus impowered and *infallible*: Is it *some few*, or *many*, or must it be the *most*? If a *few* or *many*, you profess that they may be *Hereticks*, and have not that authority or gift. If it must be *all*, or the *greater* part; 1. Then the Church of *Rome* goeth down, that is at most but a third part. 2. How shall every poor man (or any man) know which is the judgment of the major part? Can he take the Votes of all the Christian World? 3. And have all that were converted in the Apostles days and

and since; first known the Major Vote of the Christians, or were they converted by the foreknown Infallibility or Authority of the Majority? (or of the Pope?)

Some will say, we see the Madness of this Popery, but how then do you say that the *faith must be received, if not from* the Church? I answer I have told you at large in a Treatise called *The Reasons of the Christian Religion*, and briefly in a smaller Treatise called *The certainty of Christianity without Popery*

Briefly, *Judging is one thing*, and *Teaching is another thing*. Before I submit to the *Decision* of a *Judge* I must know his *Commission* or *Authority*; and I must then stand to his Sentence which way ever he decide the Case. Men be not converted to Christianity by such *Judges*, but by *Teachers*; Nor will I believe the Judge if he say *there is no Christ, no Life to come, &c.* But a *Teacher* is to make intelligible to his Hearer or Scholar, the *evidence of truth* which is in the matter taught, and to draw men to believe by telling them those true reasons upon which he did believe himself: And no man takes him for his Teacher that he is perswaded knoweth no more than himself. And the greater reputation of Knowledge and Honesty the Teacher hath, the easier we apply our minds to learn of him, and a humane trust or faith prepareth us to receive that evidence of truth which may beget a Divine Faith by the help of Grace. But still the Learner truly believeth no more than he thus learneth. And I may hear a stranger tell what he hath to say, and be convinced by the evidence that he giveth me of the truth; though I know not of any *Authority* that he hath to teach me, much less *judicially* to *decide* the Case. I little doubt but most that were converted by the Apostles themselves, were perswaded to believe in Christ by the *evidence of truth*

truth proposed (the Spirit co-operating) before they knew of any *Authority* of the Apostles; much less before they heard what they said in a *General Council*, or what was the Vote of the *Universal Church*; or what any *Pope* said as *Ruler* of the rest. These things are very plain and sure, and they that will be wilfully blinded by faction, and prejudice, and worldly interest against plain truth, have no excuse if they perish in darkness.

II. *A PAPIST (of this sort) is one that believeth that the Pope of* Rome *is the rightful Governour of all the world; that is, that all Christians immediately, and all Infidels and Heathens mediately, are bound by God to obey him, as Christs Vicegerent on Earth: And that he, with his Council, is thus an Universal Lawgiver and Judge to all Kings, States, and Persons, that dwell round about the Earth.*

But a Protestant denyeth this, and holdeth that there is no Universal Monarch, or Legislator, to all the world, but God and our Saviour; and that he hath made no such Vice-Christ, or Vicegerent; and that such a Claim is High-Treason, as usurping his Prerogative. And that if Pride had not *in tantum* made them mad, no men could think themselves thus capable of Governing all the World. Protestants believe that there is no such thing on Earth, as an Universal Church headed by any mortal Head, Pope or Council, but that Christ is the only Universal Governour or Head.

III. *This Papist is one that holdeth, that the Church of Christ on Earth is no bigger than the Popes Dominion, and that it is necessary to salvation to be subject to the Pope; and consequently he unchurcheth two or three parts of the Christian World, and damneth most of the Body of Christ, and robbeth him of the greatest part of his Kingdom, as*
far

far as denying his Right amounts to: And consequently is a notorious Schismatick or Sectary, appropriating the Church title only to his Self.

This is proved before from the Masters of their Religion.

IV. *This Papist is one that holdeth, that those Councils which were General as to one Empire, were General as to all the Christian world: And that such General Councils there must be, (if it please the Pope to call them,) though they must come from all the Quarters of the Earth, and whence they have no Sea passage, and out of the Empires of many Princes, and many that are Enemies to the Christian Name, and perhaps at Wars with Christians; and when the Voyage or Journey is such, that if the Churches be deprived of a thousand Bishops, twenty of them are never like to live to return home to the remotest Nations. Nor could they converse as a Council, by reason of the number and diversity of Languages, if they were equally gathered.*

Or they hold, that if a small part of the Christian world assemble (as at Trent*) when the rest cannot come, this is an Universal Council of and to all the Christian World.*

V. *This Papist is one that holdeth, If a fallible Pope and a fallible General Council do but agree, their Decrees are infallible: As if an unlearned Pope (e. g. that understands not the Text of Scripture in the Original) and an unlearned Council (as to the most) should agree, their Decrees would be learned; e. g. in judging which is the true Translation of a Tongue which they never understood. As if ten purblind men if they meet together might produce the Effects of the clearest sight, or Fools by conjunction become wise.*

VI. "He holdeth that Tradition from Fathers to
"Children

"Children is the sure way of conveying all the matter
"of Faith and Religion; and yet that the greatest General Councils, which are the Church representative,
"may erre in matter of Faith, and have erred; unless a
"Pope (who is fallible) approve of their Decrees.

  VII. "And when he hath trusted to this way of Tradition, he denyeth the Judgment and Tradition professed by the greater half of the Christian World.

  VIII. "He believeth that all men are bound on pain
"of damnation to believe that the Senses and perception
"of all men in the World are deceived, in apprehending
"that after Consecration there is true Bread and Wine in
"the Sacrament. And he that will so believe his own
"and others Senses, should suffer as an Heretick, and be
"rooted out of all the Dominions of all Christian Lords
"on Earth. So merciful is he to his Neighbours.

  For an approved General Council hath decreed this, and such Councils are his Religion. Were it his own Father or Mother, Wife or Child, that cannot thus renounce all his own and other mens Senses, and believe that there is no Bread or Wine in spight of his sight, taste, touch, *&c.* he believeth that they should be *burnt as Hereticks,* or *exterminated.* He may be a *good natur'd* man that is loth it should be so; or he may be one that is *ignorant* of his own Religion, and doth not know that this is one Article of Popery; or he may be an *unconscionable* man, that will not obey that which he knoweth to be his Religion; or he may be *unable* to execute such Laws: But *it is his Religion* to believe that he ought to do it.

  IX. "If he be a Temporal Lord of a Protestant Country, it is part of his Religion to take himself obliged to
"root out, destroy, or burn all his Protestant Subjects, and
"all others that deny Transubstantiation.   Obj.

Obj. *The King of* France, *and some others, do it not.*

Ans. No man is bound to do that which he *cannot do.* But if he *can do it,* and he be a *Papist,* by the express words of an Approved General Council he is bound to do it, and to *believe* that it is his duty. I speak not of what *men do,* but what their *Religion binds them to do:* Though interest or good nature hinder them.

X. "He believeth that all Temporal Lords that will "not first take an Oath thus to root out their Subjects, "and then do it, may be first Excommunicated by the "Pope, and then deposed if they repent not, and their "Dominions be given to be seized by another Papist "that will do it.

The words of the Council are before cited.

XI. "He believeth that in this case the Pope may ab- "solve all the Subjects of such Temporal Lords from "their Oaths, and Duties of Allegiance or Fidelity to "such Rulers.

This also is express in the Councils words.

XII. "He is one that believeth that the Priviledges of "the *Roman* Church were given it by the Fathers, be- "cause it was the Imperial Seat, and therefore *Constan-* "*tinople* had after equal Priviledges: (*For so saith the* "*forecited General Council:*) And yet he believeth the "clean contrary, even that *Rome*'s Priviledges were gi- "ven it by S. *Peter,* and *Constantinople*'s are not equal. (For Popes and Councils also are for this.)

XIII. "He believeth that it is *de fide* that General "Councils are above Popes, and may judge them, and "depose them if there be cause, even as Hereticks or "Infidels, Adulterers, Murderers, Simonists, *&c.* And yet "he believeth that all this is false, and the contrary "true.

Z   For

For the approved General Councils of *Basil* and *Constance* say the first, (and others;) and those fore-cited at the *Laterane* and *Florence* say the latter.

XIV. "He maketh uncharitableness, and bold damning all others, a comfortable mark of the safety of his state, and the truth of his Religion, and, our Charity a mark that ours is worse; whereas Christ hath said, *By this shall all men know that ye are my Disciples, if ye love one another.*

It's usual with them to say, [*You say that a Papist may be saved, and we say that a Protestant cannot; therefore we are in the safer state.*] As if our case were ever the more dangerous for *their* condemning us. As if a man that doteth in a Fever, should say to those about him, [*You say that I may live, and I say that all you are mortally sick; therefore my case is better than yours.*] God saith, *Judge not, that ye be not judged;* and *who art thou that judgest another mans Servant?* And these men hope their case is safe, because they sin against this Law, and damn the most of the Universal Church.

XV. "A Papist thinketh that all the Bible is not big "enough, or hath not enough in it, to save those that "believe and practise it; or to make us a saving Religi-"on; but other Tradition must be received with equal "reverence; and the Decrees of all the approved Gene-"ral Councils must make it up.

XVI. "He confesseth every Article and word of the "Religion of the Protestants to be infallibly true; and "yet holdeth that they are to be burnt and damned as "Hereticks.

For he confesseth every part of the Canonical Scripture to be true, and we have no more in our (objective, positive) Religion, not a word. Our Negations of Popery

pery are not properly our Religion, any more than our speaking against Diseases is our Health: But as our health containeth our own freedom from an hundred diseases which we never thought of, as well as those that we once had or feared; so our Faith and Religion is *free from* Popery, and containeth that which is against it.

XVII. "A Papist is for swearing men to take Scripture "in that sense as the holy Mother Church doth hold, and "hath held it: Whereas, 1. Their Church hath given "them no Commentary on the Scripture, one way or "other. 2. And their Translations have been altered in "many hundred places by *Clement* 8. and *Sixtus* 5. so "that their Clergy is sworn to take one Translation to "to be right one year, and a different one to be right "the next.

XVIII. "They are for swearing men to take or interpret Scripture but according to the unanimous sense of "the Fathers, and consequently never to interpret the "most of it at all.

XIX. "A Papist hath a thriving Faith and Religion, "which groweth bigger and bigger, as fast as General "Councils add new Decrees; so that they know not "when they shall have all: And yet they cry out against "novelty and change, and boast of Antiquity.

XX. "He holdeth that Priests or Prelates may not "fall down to Princes, or eat at their Tables, nor debase "themselves to them; but Emperours must take them "as equals. *Concil. Gen.* 8. *Const. Can.* 14.

XXI. "He is satisfied that their Church hath a Judge "of Controversies, though he decide them not: And "he gloryeth in the Unity and great Concord of their "Church, whose Doctors differ *de fide* even in the Exposition of many hundred Texts of Gods Word; and

"where they differ in the Morals before cited, about
"Murder, killing excommunicate Kings, &c. and in
"Volumes of Controversies. And yet he looketh upon
"far smaller differences among us with great offense, as
"if they were intolerable, and were so many different
"Religions: And all because in all their differences they
"agree in one Pope. As if it were not as good an Uni-
"on to agree in one God, one Christ, one Spirit, one
"Body or Church of Christ, one Faith (Creed and Scrip-
"ture) one Baptismal Covenant, and one Hope of life
"eternal, *Eph.* 4. 3, 4, 5, 6. which is the Union that
"God describeth.

XXII. "He believeth that the Pope doth justly take
"away from the People one half of the substance of
"Christs own Sacrament, and deny them that which
"they hold to be his very Blood.

XXIII. "They believe that they ought not to read the
"Scripture translated without a Licence. So saith *Con. Trid.*

XXIV. "They believe that the Image of Christ is to
"be reverenced equally with the holy Scriptures.

It is a Councils words before cited: Yea they must believe the second Council at *Nice*, that *Latria is to be given only to God*: and yet a canonized S. *Thomas* 3. q. 25.
a. 3. & 4. maintaineth that *Latria* or Divine Worship is to
be given, 1. To the Image of Christ, 2. To the Cross that
he dyed on, 3. And to the Sign of the Cross. And how
largely *Jac. Nauclautus*, *Cabrera*, and multitudes of the
Schoolmen are for it, see my *Key*, *p.* 165, &c.

XXV. "They will publickly pray to God, and praise
"him, in an unknown Tongue, because the Pope will
"have it so.

XXVI. "They think that the far greatest part of the
"Body of Christ are tormented in the Flames of Purgatory,

"tory, to make satisfaction to Gods Justice for some "Sins, notwithstanding Christs sufficient satisfaction.

XXVII. "Expecting to go to the Flames of Purgato-"ry when they dye, they cannot possibly be willing to "leave this World, and consequently must be world-"lings, and never truly willing to dye. For the basest "condition on Earth will seem to them more desirable "than Purgatory.

XXVIII. "They think that the Flames of Purgatory "do perfect mens preparation for Heaven: whereas he "is readiest for Heaven that is likest to those in Heaven "and most holy, and that is they that most love God! "And they that are angry here with every one that hurt-"eth him, and do not think that tormenting men will "win their love, yet look that the torments of Purgato-"ry should help us to love God, better than all the mer-"cies on Earth will do.

XXIX. "The generality of Papists believe a fallible "Priest, or Printer, or such other person, telling them "what is the Faith of the Universal Church, and yet "think that this is an Infallible Faith.

XXX. "A Papist is one that layeth his hopes of sal-"vation upon his belief of and obedience to a Pope "which by their own Principles is no Pope, and a Ge-"neral Council which is no General Council, never was, "nor never will be; and on his Communion with a "Catholick Church which is no Catholick Church, but "a Sect. All which hath been proved already, and more shall be.

I have told you in part what we take a Papist to be. Some things, before mentioned in the description of a Pope, have been here necessarily repeated.

CHAP.

CHAP. VIII.

What the Papists Church is: (called the Roman Catholick Church.)

WHat their CHURCH is may so easily be gathered from what is said, that I shall say but little more of it.

In General, *It is a Society called Ecclesiastical, constituted of such a Head, and such Members, as I have described.*

Particularly, I. "It is a Humane Church as to the Efficient Cause of its Form; made by Man, as distinct from that Church-form which was instituted by Christ; even by the Fathers, because that *Rome* was the Imperial Seat. As is proved before.

II. "It is a Humane Church as to the constitutive Head, as distinct from the true Universal Church, which hath no Head (single or collective, Pope or Council) that is not God.

III. "It is a Sect consisting of about the third part of the Christian world, calling themselves the whole Church, and condemning all the rest for not subjecting themselves to this Usurping Head.

IV. "It is a new Church in comparison of Christs Universal Church, as having a new Humane Original. (As is proved.)

V. "It is a treasonable Church, as set up without Christs Authority, and challenging his Prerogative, and weakning his Kingdom, by unchurching the greatest part.

VI. "It is an unholy Church, as distinct from the
"holy

"holy Catholick Church, and that both in the essential
"Matter and Form. 1. In the Matter, its Head which
"is a constitutive part, having been oft a condemned
"Heretick, Infidel, Murderer, and other flagitious wick-
"ed man. 2. As to the Form, being not of God it is
"not holy. 3. Besides that, as to the Head, he was long
"made by the most wicked Whores.

All this is before proved at large.

VII. "It is a Church that hath had its pretended suc-
"cession interrupted, (*as is proved*;) sometimes by long
"Vacancies, sometimes by long Schismes, when no one
"was the Universal Head; sometimes by the Incapacity
"of the Persons, being Lay-men, or Infidels, Simoniacal,
"condemned deposed Hereticks, and therefore no Bi-
"shops.

VIII. "It is a Schismatical Church, that cuts off it self
"from all the rest of the *Christian Church*: And by ma-
"king a false Head and Principle, and conditions of Uni-
"ty, which the *Universal Church* never did, never will,
"or can unite in, is the grand cause of the greatest con-
"tinued Schism.

IX. "It is a trayterous *Church* against Princes, ma-
"king it their very Religion to force bloody Oaths on
"them, and to excommunicate and depose them, and
"give away their Dominions, and that tolerateth its most
"famous Doctors to maintain, that being excommuni-
"cate, they are no Kings, and may be killed; and to
"maintain, that the Pope is above them in Temporals,
"and may set up and pull down Kings when he seeth
"cause.

All this is expresly proved before.

X. "It is a *Church* that believeth Contradictions (*as
"is proved in their Councils*) e.g. The Council of *Basil*,
"*Sess*.

"*Sess. ult.* saying [No one of the skilful did ever doubt,
"but that the Pope was subject to the Judgment of a
"*General Council,* in things that concern Faith, *&c.*]
"And others saying the clean contrary: As also in divers
"other things.

XI. "It was for above forty years, sometimes two,
"sometimes three *Churches,* instead of one: For the
"Head being an essential part, two or three Heads make
"as many Churches.

XII. "It is at this day divers Churches really, as to
"the Form, that are by the ignorant supposed to be one:
"Two or three Forms and *Partes Imperantes,* being essen-
"tial, make as many Churches, though the subjects live
"mixt. The *summa Potest.as* is a constitutive essential
"part. Some called Papists take the Pope for the *summa
"Potest.u,* and some a *Council,* and some both conjunct,
"and some the Church real or diffused through the
"World.

XIII. "It is a Church made up of a tolerated hodge-
"podge of many Sects, some utterly uncapable Members,
"so they do but serve the Pope.

I have shewed out of many Doctors cited by *Sancta
Clara* that many that believe not in Christ are of their
Church. He saith himself pag. 113. (*Deus, Nat. Grat.*)
["What is clearer than that at this Day, the Gospel
"bindeth not, where it is not authentically preached;
"that is, that at this Day men may be saved without an
"explicite belief of Christ? For in that sence speaks
"the Doctor concerning the Jews: And verily what e-
"ver my illustrious Master hold, with his learned Ma-
"ster *Herera,* I think that this was the Opinion of *Scotus,*
"and the COMMON one, *citing* many that fol-
"low it.

And

And that men that hold all the different Opinions in the *Jefuites Morals*, and the Schoolmen, befides many various Religious Sects, make up their Church, is not denyed.

XIV. "It is a *Church* that pretendeth to have a Judge "and end of Controverfies; but indeed hath a Judge "that for the moſt part dare not decide them, and that "can make no end of them when decided.

For inſtance, the Controverſie of the Virgins immaculate conception decided at *Bafil*, is never the nearer an end. Images were decreed up by fome *Councils*, and down by others. Even S. *Thomas* ſtood not to the ſecond *Council* of *Nice* about Image Worſhip. The various *Councils* that decreed variouſly for and againſt a *Councils Supremacy*, never the more ended the ſtrife.

And indeed it is ſo hard to know *approved* from *reprobate Councils*, and *what parts* of them the Pope meant to approve, and what not, (as by Pope *Martin* 5. his *Conciliariter* appeareth) that there is no certainty, and no end.

XV. "It is a *Church* that hath almoſt laid by the anci- "ent Diſcipline of Chriſts appointment, and inſtead of "it hath ſet up partly Auricular Confeſſion, when it "ſhould be Publick, and partly a tyrannical ſort of ho- "ſtile proclaiming their Adverſaries excommunicate "without hearing them, and forbidding Gods Word and "Worſhip to whole Kingdoms.

Saith Learned *Albaſpineus*, a Biſhop, *Obſerv*. 1. *pag*. 1. [*If ever any one in this Age was deprived of Communion (which I know not whether it ever fell out) it was only from the receiving of the Euchariſt: In the other parts of his life he retained the ſame familiarity and converſe with other Believers, which he had before he was excommuni-*
[*cated.*]   A a   XVI. "It

XVI. "It is a *Church* that is upheld by Flames and "Blood, distrusting the ancient Discipline, and the meer "Protection of the Magistrate, and the proper work of "his Office.

The foresaid 12. General Council at *Laterane* proveth it, besides Inquisitions and bloody Executions.

XVII. "It is a *Church* that cherisheth ignorance in the "matters of Salvation.

Proved, 1. By forbidding the reading of the Scriptures translated, without Licence. 2. Their Prayers in an unknown Tongue. 3. The quality of their commonest Members.

XVIII. "It is a *Church* that militateth against Christi-"an Love. 1. By their foresaid condemning the most of Christians. 2. By the foresaid bloody Religion and Execution.

XIX. "It is a *Church* which hath often damned it self, "one Pope and Council damning others. *As is proved.*

XX. "It is a *Church* which indeed is no *Church*, ac-"cording to their own Rules; the Pope indeed being no "Pope, and the General Councils no General Councils, "(*as is proved.*) And if it were one, it could not possibly "be certainly known to be so; because the Pope, who "is an essentiating part, cannot be certainly known. As is proved both as to Election, Ordination, and all that is necessary to a Right and Title.

As to the Doctrines which they hold contrary to the Scriptures, I have named many of them elsewhere, (in my *Key*, *pag.* 39, 142, 143, *&c.*) And others more largely.

And thus I have told you what I take a *Pope*, a *Papist* and the *Papal Church to be*. But you must remember that as the same man may be a visible Christian or Member

of

of the true Universal Church as headed by Christ, and a visible Papist or Member of the Sectarian Church as headed by the Pope, so I judge none of you as in the first respect, but allow you the same Charity proportionably as I do other erring Sects: And especially to those many thousands who adhere to a Church which they understand not, and profess that in gross which in particulars they themselves abhor: Of which number I am not hopeless your self (*W. H.*) to be one.

CHAP. IX.

How our Religion differeth from the Papists.

AND now out of all this it is easie for you to gather how our Religion differeth from the Papists: I shall recite but a few of the Differences, leaving you to collect the rest from what is said of theirs.

I. *Our Religion is wholly Divine, or made by God:* For so is the holy Scripture, which is all ours. *But the Papists superadditions are made by men:* Even Popes and Councils, under pretence of Declaring, Expounding, Governing, Judging, &c.

II. " The Religion of Protestants is no bigger, nor no
" other in the Essentials, than the Sacramental Covenant
" with God the Father, Son, and Holy Ghost, expoun-
" ded in the Creed, Lords Prayer, and Decalogue: And
" in the Integrals no bigger, nor other, than the holy Ca-
" nonical Scriptures. But the Papists is as big as all the
" Decrees of all General Councils, added to all the Bible;
" if not the Popes Decretals also, and uncertain Tra-
" ditions.

Tell us not of our 39 Articles, and other Church Confessions, as contrary to this: For those Confessions all profess what I here say; And you may as well tell us of our other Books and Sermons. Our question is not of mens *Subjective Religion*; For so each person hath one of his own; And it cannot be known but by knowing what is in each mans mind! And our Books and Confessions are (as is aforesaid) but the Expression of our sense of that which is our *Regular Objective Religion*: And we are ready to confess and amend any misconception: but our *Objective Religion* which is the *Rule* and *Law* of our *Faith* is only Divine.

III. "Our Religion is known, even the Sacred Bible. "But yours is unknown: what are approved Councils, "and what decrees are intended to be *ae fide*, and what "temporal, and what perpetual, and how far the Popes "Decretals bind, and whether all *Isidore Mercator*'s De-"cretals be the Popes, with abundance of the like.

IV. "Our Religion is owned by you, and every word "confessed to be Divine and Infallible: But your added "Popery is disowned by us as sinful, presumptuous and "false.

V. "Our Religion is fixed and unchangeable; (for so you confess the holy Scriptures to be:) "But yours is still "swelling bigger and bigger while Councils will increase "it, and hath no certain bounds.

VI. "Our Religion is only that ancient one delivered "by the Holy Ghost in the Apostles, and so is certainly "Apostolical, your additions are Novelties since brought "in.

VII. "Our Religion is Infallible, Holy, Pure, your "additions are fallible, contradictory, sinful, oft contrary "to plain Scripture, condemning one another.

VIII. "Our

VIII. "Our Religion is Universal, owned by all the "Christian World in the Essentials, and in the Main in "the Integrals, that is, the Scripture: Greeks, Papists, Armenians, Abassines, and all other parties that are Christians own it. "But your additions are some disowned "by one part of Cristians, and some by another, and "some by all save your selves.

IX. "Our Religion therefore is the true terms of Ca-"tholick concord, according to *Vincent. Lerinenf. Doctrine, quod ab omnibus, semper, ubique receptum est.* "But your additions are the very Engine of the dividing "Enemy, by which he hath long kept the Christian "World, distracted by discord, with all the calamitous "effects and consequents.

X. "Our Religion hath a certain Rule for the ending "of all controversies, so far as there is hope of ending "them in this world: All men will rest in the Judgment of God; and his word in all such necessary things is plainer than all your General Councils: But your Humane Authority is such as fighteth with it self and all the world, and which the Universal Church never yet received nor will ever rest in.

XI. "Our Religion owneth a certain lawful Govern-"ment appointed by God, which well used may keep "just order in the world: That is, Parents in Families, "Pastors in such particular Churches as Christ hath in-"stituted, (as join for personal Communion in holy Doctrine, Worship and Conversation;) which they are indeed capable of Overseeing and Governing by Sacred Doctrine in Christs way: And Associations or Correspondencies of these Pastors for concord; "And Prin-"ces and Magistrates to keep peace and order among "them all; Governing Clergie-men as they do Philosophers,

sophers, Physicians, &c. But yours hath an *Utopian* pretended Government of men on the other side the world, whose Countries you scarce ever heard or dreamed of; and an Usurpation of an impossible confounding kind and degree of Rule.

XII. "Our Religion is fitted to give Glory to Christ, "and his Grace and Kingdom. But yours to set up "Proud Usurpers over Princes and People, in such an "impossible Government making Subjection to him, ne-"cessary to salvation. As if a man unacquainted with Cosmography that never heard that there was such a Town as *Rome* in the world, must be no Christian and be damned: when yet the Popes name was never mentioned in our Baptism.

XIII. "Our Religion is Faith working by Love. "Christs Ministers that are truly of our Religion, take "only convincing evidence of Truth, and unfeigned "love, and works of love, to be their means of winning "Souls: And they take not Christs Discipline, which "worketh only on the conscience, to be a leaden Sword, "or vain. But yours is a hanging killing Religi-"on; Jails, Strappado's, Exterminating, and Burning "men are your means and works of love. You take a Bonfire, or the Ashes of the Bodies of such as will not believe in the Pope, to be a great Medicine to save the peoples Souls. Such Murders as were done on the *Albigenses*, *Waldenses*, in the Inquisitions, the *French* and *Irish* Massacres, *Smithfield* Flames, *Piedmont*, &c. are your proof that you love God and Man, and some of your *good works*.

XIV. "Our Religion tendeth to holy consolation, and "a heavenly mind and life: For it teacheth us how to be "certain of Gods love by its effects on our Souls, and to
"know

"know that we are justified by Chrift, and to truft the
"fufficiency of his Sacrifice, Merits, and Interceffion;
"and to believe, that when we are abfent from the body
"we fhall be prefent with the Lord, 2 *Cor.* 5. 1.7, 8. and
"to defire to depart and be with Chrift, *Phil.* 1. 23. But
yours leaveth a man uncertain of his Juftification: For
you moftly deride fuch diftinguifhed Fundamentals, as
(received) effentiate a juftified Chriftian: And your Doctors lay all mens neceffary Religion, and fo their Peace,
upon their *receipt of fo much truth as hath been authentically propofed to them*; whereas no man living is certain
that he hath received fo much as hath been fo propofed:
All men are guilty of neglecting fome fuch Propofal at
one time or other: And gradual neglects the beft are
guilty of. And you cannot afcertain men what is an authentick Propofal. You alfo tell men of the neceffity of
their own *fatisfactions* for the fin that Chrift forgiveth,
and that in the Fire of Purgatory; fo that (as is faid before) none fuch can dye comfortably, that look to go
hence into fuch a Fire, where torment may make it hard
to you to love God that tormenteth you. It is a fpirit of
bondage that feemeth to actuate your very aufterities, and
to turn your Religion into fuperftitious tasks of felf-made
Services; Ceremonies, and expectations of the expiating
Flames in Purgatory: But you fhew too little of the *Spirit of adoption, of power, love and a found mind*, 2 *Tim.*1. 7.
of *righteoufnefs, peace and joy in the Holy Ghoft*, *Rom.* 14.
Terrour and *Torments* are temptations to you to defire
the miferableft life on Earth (much more a life of pleafure) rather than to dye, when fuch Flames muft next
follow.

XV. "We offer God fuch Worfhip as we can prove
"by his Word that he commandeth and accepteth; and
"fuch

"such reasonable service in spirit and truth, which is not
"unsuitable to the Father of Spirits, and God of wisdom;
"yet using all reverent and decent behaviour of the bo-
"dy as well as of the mind. But it would be hard to
number over all the Humane inventions of *Formalities,*
and *Rites,* and *Ceremonies,* and *Images,* and other arbi-
trary external things, by which you have corrupted the
Worship of God, and hid the body in your new fashion-
ed Cloathing, which you pretended to adorn; And as
worldly minds do cumber themselves, as *Martha,* with
many unnecessary things, and then say, [*Is it not lawful
to do this and that?*] while they hereby alienate the
thoughts, affections, and time, which should be laid out on
the *one thing needful*; so do you in Gods Worship make
such abundance of work with your Ceremonies, for
thoughts, affections, and *time,* as maketh it very difficult to
give the great and spiritual part of Worship its proportion, (far beyond what *Augustine Epist. ad Januar.* so much
complained of in his time:) and then think you justifie
all, if you can say, *How prove you this or that unlawful?*
As if your Servant should instead of his work play at
Cards most of the day, and ask you [*How you prove it unlawful?*] You never well studyed 2 *Cor.* 11. 3. [*I fear
lest by any means as the Serpent beguiled Eve through his
subtilty, so your minds should be corrupted from the simplicity that is in Christ,*] nor *Col.* 2. 18, 19, 20. 22, 23. nor
Act. 15. 28. nor *Rom.* 14 and 15. nor *Joh.* 4. 20, 21. An
ignorant Woman set upon Christ, just as you pervert all
holy discourse, with turning all to [*which is the true
Church?*] *Our Fathers Worshipped in this Mountain, and
ye say that in Jerusalem is the place where men should worship:* But Christ answereth you in her, *The true Worshippers shall Worship the Father in spirit and in truth: For the
Father*

Father seeketh such to worship him: God is a Spirit, &c.] Those that by Custom be not ingaged in your way of numerous Formalities and bodily actions, can hardly think that you are spiritually and seriously worshipping God, or can believe that Infinite Wisdom would be pleased with such things as —— I am loth to denominate or describe.

XVI. " Our Religion teacheth us that without Holi-
" ness none shall see God, and none but the Pure in
" Heart and Life are blessed, and if any man have not the
" sanctifying spirit of Christ he is none of his: and that
" God must be loved above all, and our treasure, heart
" and conversation must be in Heaven, and none but
" Saints are saved. I think you deny none of this; And yet you Canonize a Saint as if he were a wonder or rarity, and you call a few sequestred Votaries *Religious*, as if all that will be saved must not be *religious*. And your Doctors are permitted to teach all that's cited in the *Jesuites Morals*, and Mr. *Clarkson* fore-cited: Even that it is not *commanded*, that *God be intensively loved above all.* *Tolet. li. 4. de Instruct. Sacerdot. c. 9.* see our *Morton Apolog. part 1. l. 2. c. 13. Stapleton l. 6. de Justif. c. 10. & Valent. l. de Votis c. 3.* [*This Precept of loving God with all the mind, is doctrinal, not obligatory.*] see my *Key*, chap. 33, 34. 38.

And yet you have the Fronts to perswade men that we are for only *Imputative Holiness*, and against *good works*.

XVII. " Our Religion is for increasing true practical
" knowledge in all men, by all our industry, as know-
" ing the Father of Lights saveth us by illumination;
" and therefore we are for all mens reading or hearing the
" holy Scriptures, and worshipping God in a known
" tongue: But yet with the help of the skilfullest Teach-
" ers.

"ers. The Prince of darkness leadeth men in the dark to do the works of darkness, that they may be cast into outer darkness. How the case is with yours I have before shewed.

XVIII. "Our Religion is for so much fasting and au-
"sterities as is truly necessary to the subduing of Pride,
"Worldliness, or fleshly lusts, or to express our self-abase-
"ment in due times of humiliation, (*prescribed by Au-*
"*thority on publick occasions, or discerned by our selves in*
"*private* ;) and so much as is truly helpful to us in Gods
"service, or our preparations for death. But how much you have turned these into unreasonable Ceremony, and how much into a pretended satisfaction to Gods Justice by punishing our selves, as if our hurt delighted God when it tends not to our healing, I shall not now stay to open. See *Dallæus de Pœnis, Indulgentis, & de Jejuniis,* of it at large.

XIX. "Our Religion teacheth us that all that truly
"believe in, and are heartily devoted to God the Father,
"Son, and Holy Ghost, as their God, and Saviour, and
"Sanctifier, forsaking the Devil, the World, and the
"Flesh, should be taken by Baptismal profession hereof
"into the Church, and shall be saved, if they prove not
"Hypocrites or Apostates: And that we must judge men
"by this their Profession, till they plainly or provedly
"nullifie it, supposing every man, under God, to be the
"best Judge of his own heart.

But your Religion teacheth you to hold and say, that if men are never so fully perswaded in themselves that they truly love God and holiness, and are thus devoted to him, yea and if their lives express it, yet if they be not Papists, they are all deceived, and none but Papists
so

so love God: And every Papist thus knoweth the hearts of others, better than we can know our own.

XX. "Our Religion leaveth us room for Repentance, "and hope of Pardon, if we mistake. For we take not our selves to be impeccable or infallible in all that we hold; though we are sure that our *Rule* and *Objective* Religion is infallible. But your Church being founded in the false conceit of the Popes and Councils Infallibility, you shut the door against repentance and amendment; and when once a false Decree is past, you take your selves obliged to defend it, lest by Reformation you pluck up your Foundation, and all should fall. Were it not for this I am perswaded your Church would recant at least the Doctrine of Transubstantiation, if not that of deposing Princes, and some others.

And now I humbly present what I have written to *W. H.* and not without hope (if he will but impartially read it) of his reduction: For the man seemeth to me to sin through Ignorance, and to have an honester zeal than many others. For my Own part, 1. I profess to him I write as I think; and that after forty years reading I think as many of the Papists Books as of the Protestants. 2. And that I would joyfully recant, whatever it cost me, if I could find that I do erre. But I have shewed him that I differ not from them, without that which to me appeareth to be constraining Reason. 3. And that if he will prove to me that I have in one word of this Book unjustly accused, either their POPE, PAPISTS, RELIGION, or CHURCH, I shall thankfully receive his conviction, and repent.

And

And I agree with him wholly in professing my Religion to be, The APOSTOLICAL CHRISTIANITY, and whatever he proveth to be truly such I will receive. The Name of [*The Protestant Religion*] I like not, because meer *Christianity* is all our *Religion*, and our *Protestation* against Popery denominateth not our Religion it self, but our Rejection of their Corruptions of it. But the Name of [*The Protestants Religion*] I approve and own, that is, APOSTOLICK CHRISTIANITY CLEANSED FROM POPERY.

Aug. 9. 1676.

FINIS.

THE CONTENTS.

CHAP. I.

Whether Chriſt hath not left us ſure and eaſie notice what the Chriſtian Religion is: what it is, and how delivered to us, in three degrees. 1. The Eſſentials generally in the Sacramental Covenant. 2. The Expoſition of the Eſſentials in three ſummaries, the Creed, Lords Prayer and Decalogue. 3. The Eſſentials, Integrals and needful Accidentals in the whole Canonical Scripture. p. 1, &c.

Our Confeſſion, Articles, Books, and Sermons are but the expreſſions of our Subjective Religion, or fides menſurata, and are not our Objective and fides menſurans in terminis. p. 9.

The Papiſts confeſs every word of our Objective Religion to be Divine and Infallible. But we confeſs not the truth of all theirs. They blame us only, 1. As not having enough. 2. And as not receiving it the right way. p. 9.

I. Whether the Papiſts Religion be better than ours, as bigger? Some Queries of the Antiquity of the belief of the Roman additions, viz. the Apocrypha and the Decrees of all the Councils, &c. p. 10, &c. What Implicite Faith we are agreed

The Contents.

agreed in, and what not. p. 12. *The Papists confess that their Church hath not kept God's own written word without many hundred errours, and so not all that is* de fide. p. 13. *Therefore they must needs distinguish the* Essentials *of Christianity from other points.*

Of Implicite belief in the Pope and Councils. p. 13. &c.

II. *Whether it was or is necessary to receive Christianity as from the Infallibility or Authority of the Pope and Papists (or Councils)* p. 19. &c. *We have much more and surer Tradition for our Religion than that which the Papists would have us trust to.* 20. *The difference of our Tradition from theirs. Whether* Rome *or a Church there may not cease.* p. 22. *Whether the Seat, the Election, or what doth prove the Pope to be St.* Peter's *successour.* p. 23. *Whether Books or oral Tradition by Memory of all Generations, be the surer preservative of the Faith.* p. 24.

CHAP. II.

THe *Puritane is ambiguously named, and falsly described.* p. 25.

Of Imputed Righteousness. p. 30. *Puritanes not against external worship, nor all Ceremonies.* p. 36. *Of their Usage,* ibid.

The Puritans judgment about Fasts Holy-days, Ceremonies, &c. p. 38. *The Papist writer knoweth not what the Puritans Religion is.* p. 40. *The true Religion of a Puritane described.* p. 41, 42. 1. *The writer wrongeth his Relations.* 2. *He declareth that he was before an ungodly perfidious Hypocrite, and no true Puritane, and therefore no wonder that he turned Papist.* p. 43.

None

The Contents.

None but such can turn Papists without self Contradiction.

His slander of the Puritanes, that they think Piety, Charity, Humility and other Christian Virtues not possible and necessary to salvation. p. 45.

CHAP. III.

His hard Character of Prelatical Protestants. p. 46. *Many Nonconformists are Episcopal; therefore not distinguishable by that name.* p. 47.

What men many Bishops and Conformists have been and are in England. p. 48.

The Religion which is uppermost, right or wrong, will be professed usually by the most, and therefore by bad men. p. 49.

It is worse with the Papists, who are many very bad, even where they differ from superiours and suffer. ibid.

His accusations of Puritanes and Prelaticks Protestants about imputed Righteousness and inherent confuted: A true description of the Protestants judgment of justifying Righteousness. p. 51, 52, &c.

His derision of Imputed Righteousness as a Mummery. p. 54, 55. *His gross slander that we are for* [meer Imputed Holiness.] p. 55.

The true middle way about Indifferent Rituals. p. 56.

1. *Of his charge on Prelatists for silencing Puritanes for not observing Fasts,* &c. *which they neglect themselves.* p. 57.

Puritanes and Papists fasting.

2. *Of wax tapers on the Altar.* p. 58.
3. *Of the Sign of the Cross.* p. 58, 59.
4. *Of the real presence.* p. 60.

The Contents.

5. *Of Confession and Absolution.* p. 61.
6. *Of bowing at the* Name Jesus, *and Images.* p. 62.
7. *Of the Surplice, Girdle, Stole, and Casuble.* p. 63.
8. *Of praying for the Dead.* p. 64.
9. *Of the Government of the Pope and Councils.* p. 65.

1. *Whether Gods Wisdom require it.* 2. *Civil and Ecclesiastick Monarchy of the whole world, Compared.* p. 66, 67. 3. *Is the Pope Universal Apostle or Teacher?* p. 55. 4. *Whether the Pope be Head but in the Vacancy of Councils?* p. 66. 5. *Most of the Christian World by far are no Papists.* 68. 6. *The Pope dissenteth from General Councils, and so far from the Universal Church: we own them when he doth not.* 69. 7. *The difference between the Kings Headship and the Popes.* 37. 8. *Puritanes are for the Kings supremacie.* 70. 9. *How far they submit their judgment to the Churches.* p. 70. 10. *The Church teacheth us the Faith, but may not judge* in partem utramlibet, viz. *that there is* no God, no Christ, no Heaven, &c. p. 71.

11. *It's Schismatical and worse to feign that various habite, Gestures, Meats, &c. make various Religions.* Q. 1. *Do variety of Liturgies make various Religions?* 2. *Is not Religion more concerned in the Papists Doctrinal Differences among themselves about Predestination, Grace, Free-will, the immaculate conception and hundreds more in the School Doctors, and about the deposing, excommunicating and killing Kings, and about all the Controversies mentioned by the Jansenists in the Jesuits Morals, and by Mr.* Clarkson *in the Practical Divinity of the Papists, than in variety of Clothes, Formes or Ceremonies? And is it not as laudable for Protestants to hold Union and Communion with them that use not the same words or rites, as in the Church*

of

The Contents.

of Rome *to tolerate without so much as any disowning censure, the foresaid Doctrinal Differences about King killing (when excommunicate) Murder, Adultery, Fornication, Perjury, Lying, Stealing,* &c. *mentioned in the foresaid Books.* p. 72.

CHAP. IV.

H. W's *ill forming Accusations, which he can best answer.* p. 77. *What* Grotius *meant by Papists.* p. 79.

I. *Of Papists Image-worship.* p. 79.
II. *Of Popes Pardons.* p. 80.
III. *Their praying to the Virgin* Mary. 83.
IV. *Latine prayers.* 84.
V. *Implicite belief in Teachers.* 85.
VI. *Preferring the Churches Laws to Gods.* 87.
VII. *Obedience.* 88.

CHAP. V.

T*He true History of the Papacie, its original and growth.* 94.

1. *The ancient Church took not the Papacie to be of Gods institution, but Mans, fully proved.* p. 99. &c.

2. *The Roman Primacie was ever but one Empire, and not all the Christian People in the world, proved.* p. 103, &c.

3. *Councils were General only as to the Empire, and not the World.* p. 104. *Five exceptions.* p. 106.

Remarks

The Contents.

Remarks upon the Africans pretended schism. (Austin being one.) p. 112. *The notable words of* Mel. Canus *against the Roman Universality.* 113.
The means of the Popes last growth to maturity. 119.
The doctrines by which they do their work. p. 122.

1. *Depressing the Scriptures sufficiency and crying up their Traditions, which are again confuted.* 123.
2. *Pretending* Antiquity *and* Universality. 125. *Both confuted. The objection of Heresie and Schism to other Churches answered.* p. 127.
3. *Aggravating our Divisions and boasting of their Unity.* p. 128.

Even the scandalous contending Sects among Protestants have more Unity with each other than the Papists, proved.

4. *Their vile Counsel to men to suspect all Religion and suspend it, to make them Papists:* Boverius *to our late King.* p. 131.

CHAP. VI.

What *the Pope is in forty Characters, or inadequate conceptions of him.* p. 134. &c.

CHAP. VII.

What *a Papist is. The word* [PAPIST] *is equivocal. Many sorts are called Papists that differ both in the* Foundation *and the very* Form *and the* Subject *and the* Terminus *of Church Power, and are not formally one Church as is commonly thought.* pag. 165.

A PAPIST *of the most learned sort described, who placeth*

The Contents.

placeth the Authority Universal *and the Infallibility in the Pope and Council agreeing:* Thirty Properties or Characters *of them. The first about the Resolution of their Faith into the Authority or Infallibility of the Church proposing. How Protestants resolve their Faith, and how they take it from their Teachers.* p. 169. &c.

See the rest.

CHAP. VIII.

What the Papists Church called the Roman Catholick Church is, in twenty Characters. p. 184.

CHAP. IX.

Twenty Properties of the Protestant's Religion as it differeth from Popery. 187.

ERRATA.

Page 26. line 28. for *Turrian* read *Pisanus*. p. 76. l. 7. for *in* r. *it*. p. 97. l. 21. r. *Presbyters*. p. 93. l. 20. r. *Roman*. p. 94. l. 2. for *or* r. *of*. p. 107. l. 1. for *Gothes* r. *Vandals*. p. 110. L. 4. dele *and*. p 115. l. 13. for *Com*. r. *Corn*. p. 123. l. 11. r. *Libraries*. p. 156. l. 28. r. *Greatreaks*.

Errata, in Roman Tradition, &c.

Page 18. l. 1. for *most real* r. *Moral*. p. 20. l. 5. r. *Georgians*. p. 29. l. 16. r. *Sirmium*. p. 37. l. 5. for *find* r. *said*.

www.ingramcontent.com/pod-product-compliance
Lightning Source LLC
Chambersburg PA
CBHW020914230426
43666CB00008B/1452